PREFACE

Evangelism: it is the lifeblood of the church of the Lord. Preachers often expound on the Christian's obligation to share the good news. Sometimes it seems that unless we have evangelistic programs, seminars or committees evangelism does not get done. This was not so in the first century.

There were no "ministers of evangelism," or evangelism seminars. There was "simply" the risen Christ and his mandate to preach the Gospel into all the world. We believe there is something missing in today's evangelistic message. What is missing is the proper understanding of the eschatological significance of the World Mission.

In the amillennial world, the past tradition of this scribe, Israel, the World Mission and eschatology are divorced from each other. The premillennialist emphasizes the World Mission and God's promises to Israel but ignores the first century context of scripture. Postmillennialism is an admixture of past and futurist views about the World Mission.

The purpose of this work is to positively set forth what the Bible says about the World Mission and the time of the end. While this is intended to be a positive work, we also examine the traditional views about Mission and Eschatology.

We want the reader to understand that while we compare the views of different men we intend no disrespect whatsoever to the commentators named herein. We do not question the sincerity of those whose views we examine. Yet we believe that their views are in error. Our desire herein is to call in question what these good men *believe*, not to impugn their motives or sincerity.

All of the elements of the World Mission need to be understood and acknowledged: the World Mission as the proclamation of the fulfillment of Israel's promises, thus, the necessity for the gospel going "to the Jew first, then the Greek"; the on-going Post-Pentecost transformation from the Old Covenant to the New; the pervasive and emphatic *first century imminence* of the time of the end; the first century fulfillment of the Commission, and the implications of realized salvation because of the fulfillment of God's promises. Only when all of these factors are understood can one truly appreciate the believer's standing and the reality of the New Creation in Christ today. We believe then that only when one understands the *past fulfillment* of the World Mission and Christ's parousia can he truly appreciate the glory of evangelism today.

In a word, the church today stands in a different place than the first century church. We stand on this side of fulfillment with the privilege of proclaiming *realized salvation*; the early church could only proclaim the imminence of that coming salvation and anticipate it with eagerness. In this scribe's view, it is far better to proclaim a realized salvation than to preach a gospel of uncertainty, delay, and fearful watching.

We ask that the reader consider this book with an open mind and Bible. The views set forth herein are admittedly controversial. *But this does not make them false.* Getting mad and calling names does not nullify evidence; nor does ignoring what is

ACKNOWLEDGEMENTS

I must express my deep appreciation to a number of people whose dedication and support have made this work possible.

To my wife for her unflagging support. I tend to be a "workaholic" and bring my work home. She is ever supportive and constant in her encouragement. In addition to her own job she has been the chief proof reader of this manuscript making many helpful suggestions.

To Scott McNeil for his cover design. Scott is one of those ever busy people, laboring at two jobs. His creative talent is great. I would like to mention my son Lance who enthusiastically involved himself in making suggestions to me.

I must also pay special tribute to the church for whom I preach, the Ardmore church of Christ. This special group of people has a great enthusiasm for the Word of God. They constantly encourage me to dig deeper. As a group, they have experienced the trauma of being ostracized for daring to challenge and reject the traditional views they once held. Yet this has only deepened their dedication to the Lord. It is a wonderful privilege to be a teacher of God's Word for these dedicated Christians.

My sincere thanks to the wonderful librarians of the Ardmore Higher Education Center. Their professional assistance in obtaining materials is an invaluable aid and makes research an exciting adventure.

I must acknowledge the many friends and fellow Bible students that have encouraged me to write. Some contributed financially, others morally, all enthusiastically. I pray that the fruit of my labor justifies their support.

My prayer is that this work will glorify the gracious God and His Son whose Scheme of Redemption is a marvel to behold, a challenge to comprehend, a joyous responsibility to teach, a blessing to experience.

Finally, this book is dedicated to the memory of my father who instilled in me a love for the Lord, respect for His Truth, and an inquiring mind with the courage to ask questions even when those questions are disturbing to self and others.

said. Only sound Biblical exegesis and logic can disprove what is offered. We welcome such scrutiny.

You may be one of the many who are disenchanted with all the frenzied prophetic speculation and repeated failure of latter day prognosticators. You may still have a deep love of God's Word but have begun to wonder if there are any true answers to the puzzling field of Biblical prophecy. You may even have become a "panmillennialist" believing "it will all *pan out* in the end"; therefore you will not think about it any more!

Whether you are a serious student of prophecy or just interested in knowing more about God's Scheme of Redemption and evangelism, this book has something to offer. We promise you a challenging adventure that hopefully will provoke even deeper study of God's Word.

Don K. Preston

FOREWORD

In most discussions of eschatology, the future of Israel has been and must always be predominate. Today, perhaps as never before, questions old and new are being asked about Israel's place in God's scheme of redemption. Is Israel's Old Testament past simply past, or does there remain a mysterious restoration in the likeness of their former distinctive nationhood?

In this book Don Preston makes an approach to the "latter days" that demonstrates beyond reasonable doubt that the Bible is a Book of God's covenant with Israel, and that its message is dated by Israel's history and its full Christological consummation in A.D. 70. To this end Christ enters the world of His brethren, carries forth His earthly ministry, and approaches the cross preoccupied with Israel's end destiny; a destiny that He sees in the immediate future. In the context of His death/resurrection departure, Christ communicates this future to His apostles in His Olivet Discourse. He instructed and prepared them for their ministry of testifying to the whole world the soteriological significance and outreach of the approaching consummation, not for Israel's benefit only, but for the benefit of "all families of the earth" who thereby were being enabled to become "partakers of Israel's spiritual things."

Preston does an impressive work in correlating the Matthew 28 commission [commonly called the Great Commission] and the disclosing ministry of the Holy Spirit, showing their relevance to Israel's "latter days" as foretold by the prophets.

In sound, systematic, exegetical fashion Preston draws from the apostle's writings invincible evidence that they held firmly to the identical imminent future that Christ had set before them, being fully conscious of their own time as the "last days." They labored with the conviction and understanding that already the powers of "the age to come" were being witnessed and experienced in advance of the end; that their message was not about some far-distant "last generation" of **mankind**, rather, the "last generation" of Israel's earthly commonwealth. And they viewed the outpouring of the Holy Spirit [Joel 2; Acts 2], and the spiritual crisis through which they were passing [Daniel 12; 1 Peter 1:6-7] from this perspective.

     We believe this book will be extremely helpful to the serious student of the Bible who is searching for a true, Biblical understanding of the meaning of Israel's future, and the time, place, and manner of its realization in Christ. After its reading is completed, it should be evident that it is the prognostications of futurist eschatologists regarding Israel's future that truly diminishes Israel. Preston's work is a strong refutation of the "anti-Semitic" label that some presume to stamp on Realized Covenant Eschatology, which in truth grants unto Israel the glory, the beauty, and the power of her promised new covenant destiny in Christ. And whatever is withheld from Israel also represents a diminishing of the "fullness of the Gentiles" and their [our!] new covenant status in Christ.

Max R. King

TABLE OF CONTENTS

CHAPTER 1 1
WAS THE PREDICTION EVER FULFILLED?
"World" a Word Study/ Two Commissions or One?

CHAPTER 2 9
THIS GENERATION SHALL NOT PASS
"Genea" a Word Study/ John the Immerser and "This Generation"/ Look at the Signs!/ The Great Day of the Lord/ The Abomination of Desolation and "This Generation"/ The Man of Sin and "This Generation"/ The Restrainer and "This Generation"

CHAPTER 3 30
WHAT ABOUT THE END OF THE AGE?
"This Age" and "The Age to Come"/ "suntelias ton aionon," A Word Study/ Defining "The Last Days"

CHAPTER 4 56
THE WORLD MISSION AND THE END OF THE OLD LAW
Matthew 5:17-18/ All Had to be Fulfilled/ Gentile Conversion Before the End/ The Fulfillment of Israel's Promises/ Romans 11:25-26 and the End of the Law/ Israel Rejected for Persecuting the Church

CHAPTER 5 72
THE WORLD MISSION, MIRACLES, AND THE END OF THE AGE
Joel 2:28: The Key to Pneumatology/ The Holy Spirit and Eschatology/ Tongues are a Sign!/ The Holy Spirit and World Mission

CHAPTER 6 85
WHAT ABOUT THE COMING OF THE LORD?
Predicted for First Century/ Understanding the Language/ The Old Testament Source of New Testament Eschatology/ The Deity of Jesus and His Coming

CHAPTER 7 94
THE PREACHING AND THE END: A CLOSER LOOK
Preaching, Persecution, Power, Parousia!/ The Lord Is at Hand!/ To Every Creature under Heaven!/ Powerful Parallels!/ The Time for the Judgment Has Come!/ Revelation: The Expanded Olivet Discourse

CHAPTER 8 119
IMPLICATIONS OF FULFILLMENT
For the Amillennialist/ For the Postmillennialist/ For the Premillennialist/ Take Inspiration Seriously/ Evangelism Today

CHAPTER 1

INTO ALL THE WORLD THEN COMES THE END!

© 1996 Don K. Preston
DKPret@aol.com

One of the most common and popular religious beliefs today is the view that the Gospel must be preached into all the world. When this is accomplished Christ will return. This belief is based upon Jesus' prediction in Matthew 24:14:

"This gospel of the kingdom must be preached in all the world for a witness to the nations, then comes the end."

Almost all premillennialists[1] would agree with Hal Lindsey's statement concerning this prediction "No one has done that yet."[2] From Paul Crouch, Jack Van Empe, Pat Robertson and others comes the message that the gospel will finally be preached into all the world in this generation and therefore this must be the generation of Jesus' return.

What would it mean if the gospel had already been preached into all the world? What would it mean for all these modern prognosticators of Jesus' return? What would it mean to *you*?

If the gospel has been preached into all the world then the modern claim that Jesus' prediction has never been fulfilled is false.

Mission Accomplished!

If Jesus' prediction has been fulfilled then Jesus is vindicated as the Son of God, we can trust the Bible as true, and salvation has come to reality.

If the gospel has been preached into all the world as Jesus said then surely "the end" must have come! Jesus certainly did not indicate a long delay between fulfillment of the World Commission and the end; he said "the gospel will be preached in all the world, *then comes the end.*"

The question then, "was the Great Commission ever fulfilled?," is a vital question for the modern church. We will show that Jesus gave a very firm time frame for the fulfillment of his prediction and that this time frame was correct. This work will show that Jesus' prediction was indeed fulfilled. We will also define what "the end" was that Jesus was predicting.

WAS THE PREDICTION FULFILLED?

Has the Great Commission been fulfilled? The millennialist says no. The amillennialist[3] and the postmillennialist[4] say TWO Great Commissions were given- Matthew 24:14 has been fulfilled but Matthew 28:18ff is another and is not fulfilled. Were there two Great Commissions? Does one Commission stand fulfilled while another is not?

First, notice the comparison below. Jesus commanded the gospel to be preached to all the world. He used a distinctive word "preach." Paul

Mission Accomplished!

used the identical word to say the gospel had been preached to all the world.

Command	Fulfillment
Matthew 24:14	Colossians 1:23
Gospel shall be "preached"	gospel was "preached"
Greek-keruxthesetai	Greek-keruxthentos
future tense	aorist [past] tense

    The only difference between Matthew 24 and Colossians is that in Matthew it is future--in Colossians it is past tense!

    Now notice the chart that lists all the passages containing the prophecy/command of the Commission being taken into all the "world," all the "earth," etc. on the left, and the passages containing the fulfillment on the right.

Mission Accomplished!

Prophecy/command	Fulfillment
In all the world Matt. 24:14-Greek-*oikoumene*	In all the world Rom. 10:18-Greek-*oikoumene*
Into all the world Mark 16:15-Greek-*kosmos*	Into all the world Col. 1:6-Greek-*kosmos*
To all creation Mark 16:15-Greek-*ktisis*	In all creation Col. 1:23-Greek-*ktisis*
Teach all nations Matt. 28:19 Greek-*ethnos*	Made known to all the nations-Rm. 16:26 Greek-*ethnos*
Judea, Samaria, world Acts 1:8 Greek-*ge*	Into all earth Rom. 10:18 Greek-*ge*

  Every word used by the Spirit to describe the scope of the Great Commission is also used by the Spirit to describe the *fulfillment* of Jesus' mandate! Yet, some still maintain the Great Commission of Matthew 24:14 has never been fulfilled! Is it not presumptuous to say a prophecy has not been fulfilled even though every term, every word employed in the *command and prediction* of that event is used by the inspired writers to say the prediction has been fulfilled?

Mission Accomplished!

To maintain therefore that the Great Commission has never been fulfilled one must deny the emphatic statements of scripture. He must insist that the "world" in Matthew meant something for *our modern world,* but that the word "world" in Romans, Colossians, etc. meant something totally different! Where is the consistency in such an interpretation?

Not only must the millennialist redefine "world" in Paul's writings, he must assume that Paul either did not know about Jesus' prediction, or if he did know of it he was redefining Jesus' words without any indication he was doing so.

Paul either knew of Jesus' prediction or he did not. If he did not know one can only marvel at such a lack of knowledge on the part of the apostle who received his gospel from the Lord himself, Gal. 1. If he did not, it is an incredible coincidence that he emphasized the preaching into all the world and used the identical words as Jesus.

If Paul *knew* of Jesus' mandate and was changing the meaning of Jesus' words how do we know this? He did not *say* he meant a different world had heard the gospel than that envisioned by Jesus! He did not use different words to indicate a smaller world than the one Jesus had in mind.

If a person can insist that *Jesus* meant the world as defined in the *twentieth century*, but that *Paul* meant the world as defined in the *first century*, what is to keep someone else from claiming that in reality Jesus had the world of the *50th century* in mind? Maybe, to be hypothetical, Jesus had in mind a world when other planets have been colonized?

If a person can so change the meaning of Biblical words to fit preconceived ideas then such manipulations cannot be rejected. Once "hidden meanings" begin to be suggested for Biblical words and terms, Biblical interpretation becomes hopelessly capricious and subjective. The only proper way to interpret scripture is to define Biblical words in the way the Biblical writers used them, not in the way modern man defines them.

The only reason to suggest that the "world" Paul said had heard the gospel was different than that spoken of by Jesus is theological necessity. When a person has a preconceived idea that something must happen in a certain way, be of a certain nature, and fulfill his/her expectations, then Biblical language only stands in the way. Such is the case when we deny that the Great Commission was truly fulfilled in the first century.

The premillennialist rightly sees the connection between the completion of the World Mission and eschatology. The amillennialist sees no such connection. The amillennialist admits, based upon Matthew 24:14, that the completion of the World Mission was related to the end of Israel in A.D. 70. But he then insists the Commission in Matthew 28:18f is unrelated to eschatology.

There is however, no such distinction between Matthew 24 and Matthew 28. This is a false dichotomy created out of theological necessity, not scriptural exegesis. Camp convincingly shows that the end of the age in Matthew 28 is the same as in chapter 24. He also shows that Jesus' promise "I will be with you" in 28:18f was the identical promise of the miraculous as found in Mark 13:9f.[5] Coupled with the study of the term "end of the age" below, it is untenable to say there were two Great Commissions, given to the same generation of disciples concerning two ends of two different ages.

The truth is, the completion of the Great Commission was *a sign of the end of the age*. As Robert Smith has succinctly stated: "The universal mission of the church [from the perspective of the New Testament writers, DKP] is no substitute for eschatology... it is a piece of eschatology. It is one sign of the end. These post-resurrection days are now the last days, foretold by the prophets [Acts 3:24; 2:17-18], which stand immediately before the Great and Terrible Day of the Lord [Acts 2:20; 17:31]."[6] For the amillennialist to deny this is to deny the plain words of Jesus.

> Jesus did not give a Great Commission and then a *Greater* Commission!

The amillennialists and postmillennialists believe Matthew 24:14 was fulfilled but Matthew 28:19 has NOT been fulfilled. Joseph Balyeat insists Matthew 28:19 is "a much more comprehensive mission than that expressed in Matthew 24:14."[7] But he offers not one scripture as proof for this assertion! Where is the evidence for delineating between Matthew 24:14 and 28:19? The same word

Mission Accomplished!

for nations is used by Jesus in Matthew 24:14 and Matthew 28:18. In Matthew 24 he *predicted what would be done*; in Matthew 28 he *commanded it to be done*. In Romans 16:25-26 Paul, using the same words, *said it had been done!* There are not two different Commissions of two gospels, or two different Commissions of the one gospel!

Are we to believe that Jesus had the end of two different ages in mind? Were there to be *two different gospels* preached into all the world for a sign of the impending end of two ages? Or was there to be one gospel and two ends of two ages? Was the end of one age the end of a Covenant Age but the end of the other to be the end of material creation? No, there was *one gospel, one Mission*, one end of *the age*. And that gospel was preached into all the world in the first century.

What more emphatic proof is needed to accept the fact that Jesus' mandate of world evangelism was fulfilled? As Kik succinctly comments "Those who would deny this must quarrel with the statements of Scriptures. All nations of the world heard the Gospel proclaimed before the year 70 AD."[8]

CHAPTER 2

THIS GENERATION SHALL NOT PASS...

To maintain that the Great Commission was fulfilled in the first century is in perfect harmony with Jesus' emphatic prediction. In Matthew 24:34 the Lord said:

"Verily I say unto you, This generation shall by no means pass away, till all these things be fulfilled."

Because of preconceived ideas many refuse to accept Jesus' inspired words. There are a number of different ways that Bible students seek to escape the seemingly obvious fact that Jesus said the Great Commission, along with the other signs he gave, and his coming in glory, would occur in that generation. Most attempts to escape the force of his words center around the term "this generation."

It is maintained that the word "genea" means "race of people" and that Jesus was actually saying the Jewish nation would not pass away until all the things he foretold came to pass.[9] But the reason for rendering generation as race is less than convincing.

The source just cited gives only one reason for rendering genea as race "when we ask the question as to whether 'all these things' really did take place at the time of the overthrow of Jerusalem by Titus in A.D. 70; whether the gospel of the kingdom had been preached in all the world, whether the Son of Man had come in the clouds in visible glory, and whether the elect had been gathered from the four winds, history answers that nothing of the kind ever occurred at that time."[10] In other words, what Jesus predicted did not happen, according to the writer's view of things, therefore he will alter the definition of Jesus' words! Here is a classic example of preconceived ideas governing the definition of words.

While the root meaning of genea may mean race, it should be noted that Bauer's Arndt and Gingrich Lexicon, [greek dictionary] does not list a single example of genea being defined that way in the New Testament. See also Balz-Schneider, etc.

In Matthew 1 we find the genealogy of Jesus. The writer says "so the generations from Abraham to David are fourteen generations; and from David until the carrying away into Babylon are fourteen generations and from the carrying away into Babylon unto Christ are fourteen generations" vs. 17. As William Bell has noted, if genea means race of people this poses severe problems in this text. It means "there would be forty-two races of the nation of Israel alone, all with the common ancestor of Abraham. Such is unforgivable exegesis."[11]

The word genea appears a total of 43 times in the New Testament.[12] The term "this generation" appears 12 times, not counting parallel passages. In each of these passages "this generation" invariably refers to the people living at the same time.

This Generation Shall Not Pass...!

An excellent example of this is found in a passage related to Matthew 24:34. In Matthew 23:29-39 Jesus condemned the Jews of his day for their recalcitrance. He predicted coming judgment in the following words:

> "Truly I say unto you, all these things shall come upon this generation."

Hal Lindsey says this verse referred to "the global dispersion" of the Jews and occurred to "the same generation that crucified Him."[13] In other words, Lindsey recognized that "this generation" was not a reference to a race of people but to the contemporaries of Jesus!

The term "this generation" in Matthew 23 is the identical term as in 24:34. How is it possible to so radically alter the meaning of a term from verse to verse. How can one admit that "this generation" in 23:36 refers to the judgment coming against Israel in the lifetime of Jesus' contemporaries, i.e., that generation, and then a few verses later, even though the subject matter is the same, insist that the identical term has nothing to do with time? In what follows below we hope to show that the term can mean nothing except Jesus' contemporary generation.

JOHN THE IMMERSER AND "THIS GENERATION"

It may just be that in the study of eschatology, the significance of John the Immerser is one of the most ignored or overlooked subjects in the entirety of the New Testament. There is much we would like to say about this but space forbids. We will limit our comments to showing that John, as Elijah, was eschatologically significant and that his ministry lends powerful credence to the claim that when Jesus said the end was to be in his generation he meant his contemporary generation.

Malachi 4:5-6 predicted the coming of Elijah before the Great and Terrible Day of the Lord at the consummation of the Last Days. In no uncertain terms, Jesus identified John the Immerser as Elijah, Matthew 11:13-14; 17:10-13. There can be no debate therefore that John was an eschatological figure heralding the coming Day of the Lord. John was a sign that the last days had come! This is powerfully confirmed by his message.

> John the Immerser is one of the most significant yet ignored or overlooked eschatological figures in the entire Bible!

John was a *Covenant Messenger*. In Malachi we are told that Elijah's message would be "remember the Law of Moses my servant" and that John's task would be to "turn the hearts of the children to the fathers and the hearts of the fathers to the children" 4:5-6. According to Malachi 3:1 he

John the Immerser and "This Generation"

was to be the messenger to prepare the way for the coming of the Lord in judgment, the time when no one could stand before that awesome presence, 3:2.

This distinctly covenantal framework for the ministry of John as Elijah is important because it gives a direct hint for identifying the Great and Terrible Day of the Lord. John was not a messenger to the nations proclaiming the end of time. He was a messenger to Israel proclaiming God's *coming to His temple in judgment, 3:1.* This should not and cannot be construed to have no significance for "all nations" for in scripture the judgment of the nations is inextricably linked with the time of Israel's judgment, Isaiah 65-66; Joel 2-3, etc. This said however, we must emphasize again that to ignore the Old Covenant framework of John's ministry is to totally misconstrue his message and the impending judgment he proclaimed. John was declaring Israel's judgment for disobedience *to her Covenant,* not the end of the Christian Age, cf. Isaiah 24; Malachi 4:6.

We must take note of the singular nature of John's message and ministry. John, so far as the record is concerned, did not declare two Great Days of the Lord, one imminent, the other protracted. He did not proclaim the Great Day of the Lord and then the *Greater Day* of the Lord. He did not teach of a "wrath about to come" and then a "greater wrath--the really big one--that will eventually come one of these days by and by." His message was about *"the wrath* about to come." It is therefore "eisegesis" of the worst sort to ignore the imminence

John the Immerser and "This Generation"

of John's preaching and extract from it a still future judgment; or to distort his preaching into "timeless imminence"; or to insist that he did foresee two Great Days of the Lord. This brings us to consider closer the imminence factor in John's message.

John's message included two aspects, "the kingdom of heaven is at hand" and "the wrath about to come." In Matthew 16:27 Jesus said he was coming *in judgment*; in verse 28 he told his audience that all of them would not die before they saw him coming *in his kingdom*. The amillennialist traditionally places a 2000 year gap between verse 27 and 28 insisting that Christ's coming in judgment and his coming in the kingdom are unrelated events.[14] But Daniel 7, Matthew 25:31f, Luke 21:25-31, and 2 Timothy 4:1, and other texts belie this.

Daniel 7:13-14 is traditionally appealed to by amillennialists as applying to the establishment of the kingdom on Pentecost. Yet Daniel 7 posits the establishment of the kingdom at the time of the coming of the Son of Man on the clouds of heaven-- *in judgment*, Daniel 7:9f; 26-27! In Matthew 25 we find the coming of the Lord in judgment and entrance into the kingdom. In Luke 21 we find the coming of the Lord and the coming of the kingdom. In Timothy we have the coming of the Lord in judgment and the coming of the kingdom. Since John proclaimed "the kingdom of heaven is at hand" he was saying that judgment was at hand!

How imminent did John foresee this kingdom/judgment to be? Robertson's comments are appropriate: "It was a startling word that John thundered over the hills and it re-echoed throughout the land. The Old Testament prophets had said that it would come some day in God's own time. John proclaims as the herald of the new day that it has come, has drawn near. How near he does not say, but he evidently means very near, so near that one could see the signs and the proof."[15] Robertson has correctly noted the tense of the Greek.

When John said the kingdom is "at hand" he literally said "the kingdom *has drawn near*"; what had once been far off had now come near, compare 1 Peter 1:5-12. Notice now James 5:8 where the inspired writer said "the coming of the Lord [parousia] has drawn near." James uses the identical Greek word rendered "at hand" in the same tense as the Immerser. Just as John proclaimed the true imminence of the kingdom, the epistles declared the true imminence of the coming of the Lord in judgment. The reason is simple: judgment and kingdom are Siamese twins linked at the heart. They cannot be separated.

It is interesting that many commentators insist that we honor John's statements about the imminence of the kingdom, yet these same commentators ignore the imminence of the judgment John was proclaiming! But since the kingdom and judgment are inseparably linked this is indefensible. John's message was of the imminent coming of the kingdom and the attendant judgment.

John the Immerser and "This Generation"

When the Pharisees and Sadducees came out to be baptized, John, knowing their hearts castigated them "Who hath warned you to flee from the wrath to come?" The word "come" or coming is from the word *mello* [tes mellouses orges]. The primary definition of this word means to be "about to, to be on the point of."[16] As Hagner says: "John's apocalyptic message involves imminent judgment of the unrighteous in *tes mellouses orges*, 'the coming wrath.'"[17] Since John was Elijah with the task of warning people of the Great and Terrible Day of the Lord, and since he told his audience that wrath was "about to come" then the Great and Terrible Day of the Lord was imminent!

The imminence factor is enhanced further in the text. John was to prepare the way for the Great and Terrible Day of the Lord. Jesus' incarnation, the time of his hiddenness and humility as the Suffering Servant, Isaiah 42; 53, is not in view here. It is the time of Jesus' parousia as the judge bringing vengeance, Isaiah 59:16-21.

John said of Jesus' judgment "his winnowing fork is in his hand, and he will thoroughly purge his threshing floor and gather his wheat into the barn" vs. 12. Notice that John presents Jesus as already holding the instruments of harvest and judgment. Compare this image of imminent *harvest* with our comments elsewhere in this work about Matthew 13 and harvest at the end of the age. This graphic imagery shows that John certainly did not perceive of any gap of thousands of years between his

John the Immerser and "This Generation"

ministry and Jesus' coming in judgment. His own presence as Elijah belies this idea. Elijah was to come before--not centuries or millennia before--the Great and Terrible Day of the Lord.

⬇ John's words were spoken before Jesus officially entered into his public ministry. Yet John saw Jesus' coming in judgment as so imminent that he said the instruments of harvest were already in his hands. It simply will not do to say that John was being given a panoramic view of history from Jesus' personal ministry until the end of time. John as Elijah was *a sign of the Day of the Lord*; he said the wrath was "about to come"; he said "the axe is already at the root" vs. 10.

The fact that John was to herald the coming of Christ *in judgment* is also apparent from Isaiah 40. This is the prophetic text that predicted the one who would be "the voice of one crying in the wilderness: Prepare the way of the Lord; Make straight in the desert a highway for our God." It is unfortunate that this is normally applied exclusively to John's message heralding Jesus' entrance into his public ministry. But such is not the context.

In Isaiah 40:5 we find that "the glory of the Lord shall be revealed and all flesh shall see it together." [Reminds you of Matthew 24:30 doesn't it? And if it doesn't it should!] It is at this coming that "The Lord God shall come with a strong hand, and his arm shall rule for Him; Behold, His reward is with Him, and His work before Him." This is undeniably a reference to Christ's coming in

John the Immerser and "This Generation"

judgment, not humility. This is the coming Jesus predicted in Matthew 16:27-28: "The Son of Man shall come in the glory of his Father with His angels, then He will reward each according to his works. Assuredly I say to you, there are some standing here who shall not taste death till they see the Son of Man coming in His glory."

John the Immerser was to be the sign and herald of this judgment coming. His words exude imminence from every syllable. The kingdom/judgment "has drawn near." He challenged his audience "who has warned you to flee from the wrath about to come?" He declared "the axe is already at the root"; "his winnowing fork is already in his hand." To discount or ignore all these statements of imminence is to do a gross disservice to Biblical interpretation. John's message is strong evidence indeed that when Jesus said the end would come in his generation he was speaking of his contemporary generation!

JUST LOOK AT THE SIGNS!

There simply is no way to deny that John as Elijah was a *sign* that the last days had come and the Day of the Lord was imminent; that was to be "Elijah's" mission! Now notice that John said Jesus would baptize with the Holy Spirit, Matthew 3:11. As we show in greater detail below, the outpouring of the Spirit was an eschatological sign of the last days before the Great and Terrible Day of the Lord,

John the Immerser and "This Generation"

Joel 2:28-32. When asked about the sign of the end Jesus gave two very specific signs of imminence: the World Mission and the Abomination of Desolation, Matthew 24:14-15. And remember, he said the World Mission and the Abomination would occur in his generation. We are contending that "this generation" was Jesus' first century contemporaries. Watch the flow.

John, as Elijah, was *a sign* of the coming of the Great Day of the Lord. He appeared in *Jesus' contemporary generation* and declared *imminent judgment*. The *Holy Spirit, a sign* of the coming of the Great Day of the Lord, was poured out in *Jesus' contemporary generation*, Acts 2. The *World Mission, a sign* of the end was fulfilled in *Jesus' contemporary generation*, Colossians 1:23. The *Abomination of Desolation, a sign* of the coming of Christ and the end of the age, appeared in *Jesus' contemporary generation*, see below. Now since *the signs* of the Great Day of the Lord undeniably appeared in Jesus' contemporary generation, his "this generation," upon what basis do we deny that "the end" came in his "this generation" just as he predicted? How can it be denied that Jesus' generation was the one he had in mind when he said "this generation shall not pass till all these things be fulfilled"?

THE GREAT DAY OF THE LORD

John was the herald and sign of the Great Day of the Lord, and the outpouring of the Spirit was a sign of that impending event as well. Another text helps us identify the nature of that event and further pinpoint the contemporary nature of Jesus' "this generation" prediction. In Revelation 6:9f John beheld the:

> "souls of those who had been slain for the word of God and for the testimony which they held. They cried with a loud voice saying: 'How long, O Lord, holy and true, until You judge and avenge us on those who are on the earth?' And a white robe was given to each of them: and it was said to them that they should rest a little while longer, until both the number of their fellow servants and their brethren, who should be killed as they were, was completed."

God's response to their prayer is in verses 12-17--the Great and Terrible Day of the Lord. Thus, the Great and Terrible Day of the Lord would be the time when the martyrs of God would be vindicated.

In Matthew 23:29f Jesus accused the Jews of being the slayers of the prophets: "which of the prophets have you not slain?" To those gathered

John the Immerser and "This Generation"

around him with blood in their eyes and hatred in their heart he said that they would "fill up then the measure of your fathers" by slaying the "prophets, wise men and scribes" that he would send to them.

In some of the more challenging words from the Master's lips he then said "upon you will come all the blood of all the righteous from Abel to Zacharias, whom you slew between the Temple and the altar." Please take note that this judgment is a universal judgment; it extends all the way back to Creation and encompasses vindication of all the righteous! Can Jesus be speaking of anything other than the judgment of the "living and the dead"? He said "upon you"--that is the living, will "come all the blood of all the righteous"--that is the dead!

Did Jesus say when this judgment would occur? His words are emphatic "Verily I say to you, all these things shall come upon this generation." As we have already seen, many premillennialists admit that in this text "this generation" speaks of Jesus' contemporary generation. Lindsey even admits that the judgment of the dispersion referred to the A.D. 70 judgment on Israel. But this text does not just mention a dispersion! It mentions the vindication/judgment of all the dead all the way back to Creation! This is the time of the end; it is the Day of the Lord!

The martyrs of God would be vindicated/judged at the Great Day of the Lord, Revelation 6. Jesus said the martyrs of God would be vindicated in "this generation," Matthew 23:36.

John the Immerser and "This Generation"

But Matthew 23:36 speaks of Jesus' contemporary generation. Therefore, the martyrs of God would be vindicated in Jesus' contemporary generation.

Since John the Immerser was the sign and herald of the Great Day of the Lord, the Day of God's Wrath, and he said it was imminent, Matthew 3, then the interrelationship of Matthew 23 and Revelation 6 to the Great Day of God's Wrath all but irrefutably confirms the definition of "this generation" as Jesus' contemporary generation. Unless one wishes to delineate between the judgment of Matthew 23 and Matthew 24:29f then this definition would seem to be beyond controversy. But such a delineation is untenable.

In Matthew 24:29f Jesus is citing Joel 2:28f-- "the sun shall be darkened, the moon shall be turned to blood...." This is the prediction of events of the Great and Terrible Day of the Lord. Thus, in Matthew 24:34, when Jesus said "this generation shall not pass till all these things be fulfilled" *he was saying that the Great Day of the Lord was for his generation.*

In Matthew 23:36 he said the vindication of all the martyrs would be in his generation and this vindication would be the Great Day of the Lord. In chapter 24 he quotes from Joel's prediction of the coming of the Great Day of the Lord and said it would be in his generation. Thus, Matthew 23 and Matthew 24 both predicted the Great and Terrible Day of the Lord, *and both texts said it would be in "this generation!"*

The Abomination of Desolation and "This Generation"

Is it not just a little strange and totally inconsistent that so many exegetes are willing to grant the first century application of chapter 23 but seek to radically redefine the term "this generation" in chapter 24? Would it not be far better to honor the Biblical definition of "this generation"? It meant the time of Jesus' contemporaries. The following study will add even more validity to this assertion.

THE ABOMINATION OF DESOLATION AND "THIS GENERATION"

Significant support that "this generation" referred to Jesus' contemporaries is the study of the Abomination of Desolation. While an entire volume could be written on this topic alone, a few facts must suffice. Jesus told his disciples:

> "when you see the Abomination of Desolation spoken of by Daniel the prophet, let him who reads understand, then let them which be in Judea flee into the mountains." Mat. 24:15-16

This prediction too is qualified by Jesus' statement that it would occur in "this generation."

Jesus told his disciples to flee to the mountains when they saw the Abomination of Desolation. He said those events would occur in his generation. If therefore we can find evidence that

The Abomination of Desolation and "This Generation"

the first century church did flee Jerusalem "en masse," then we not only have prima facia evidence for the identity of the Abomination of Desolation but we find confirmation of the temporal meaning of "this generation."

The church historian Eusebius, [270-340 A. D.], records:

> "The whole body, of the church at Jerusalem, having been commanded by a divine revelation, given to men of approved piety there before the war, removed from the city, and dwelt at a certain town beyond the Jordan, called Pella."[18]

The Encyclopedia Judaica concurs with this testimony: "The small Christian community remained in Jerusalem until 66 A.D., when it retired to Pella."[19]

Just as Jesus urged his disciples departed Jerusalem. Since Jesus told his contemporary disciples what to do when they saw the Abomination of Desolation, and they did it just prior to the fall of Jerusalem, this is strong evidence indeed that "this generation" meant Jesus' generation.

Was the early church not obeying Jesus' mandate? Were they not seeing the Abomination of Desolation?[20] If not, why were their actions perfectly consistent with Jesus' commands in regard to the Abomination? Were their actions and Jesus' words just a strange combination of coincidence?

The Abomination of Desolation and "This Generation"

If that generation was not the generation Jesus had in mind, is it not strange that the disciples did what Jesus predicted to be done in the critical generation? Is it not strange also that if that generation was not the generation to see the preaching of the gospel to all the world that the New Testament is so adamant that it *was preached* to all the world?

Finally, we have additional evidence that the Abomination of Desolation occurred in Jesus' contemporary generation and that evidence also gives us further insight into the eschatological significance of the World Mission.

It is widely agreed that the Man of Sin in 2 Thessalonians 2 is associated with, even if not identified as the same as, the Abomination of Desolation. Our purpose is not to identify the Abomination or the Man of Sin but rather to take note of the chronological indicators in the text.

In verses 6-7 the apostle speaks of the Man of Sin as a contemporary reality being restrained even as he wrote. The Man of Sin was being restrained in the first century! In verse 7 Paul said "the mystery of iniquity is already at work." There is not the slightest indication that the apostle is contemplating the passing of centuries before the Abomination would be revealed. There is not a hint that the restraining thing, or the restraining one, was not already restraining the Man of Sin--there is the direct opposite. The restraining thing and the restraining one were even then holding back the

The Abomination of Desolation and "This Generation"

manifestation of the Man of Sin. Now if the restrainer was at work then the Man of Sin was present! It is a little difficult to restrain something that is not present.

These chronological indicators agree perfectly well with the historical information above. Further, the parallels between Matthew 24 and 2 Thessalonians coupled with the temporal statements all but forces us to acknowledge the first century application of these texts.

Jesus said men would come saying the Lord had come, Matthew 24:26f; Paul told the Thessalonians not to be deceived that the Day of the Lord had come, 2 Thessalonians 2:2. Jesus told his disciples to flee *Judea* when they saw the Abomination of Desolation; Paul said the Man of Sin would establish himself in the Temple of God, 2:2:4. Jesus warned of the false teachers that would perform false miracles to lead astray the elect; Paul said the Man of Sin would perform false miracles, 2:2:9. Jesus foretold his coming, [*parousia*]; Paul is speaking of the coming [*parousia*] of the Lord, 2:2:1. Jesus predicted the gathering [episunagogee] of the elect; Paul is speaking of the gathering together [episunagogee] to Christ. Jesus predicted his coming at the height of the Abomination of Desolation; Paul said the Man of Sin would be destroyed by the coming of the Lord, 2:2:8. Jesus said his coming would be in "this generation"; Paul said the Man of Sin was already present.

In other words, what Jesus said would take place in his generation was beginning to unfold even

The Abomination of Desolation and "This Generation"

as Paul wrote. This is powerful evidence that Jesus' reference to "this generation" was indeed his contemporary generation.

THAT WHICH RESTRAINS:
HE WHO RESTRAINS

The significance of the World Mission is also evidenced from this Thessalonian text. Scholars have long debated the identity of the Restrainer. The Restrainer has been identified as the Holy Spirit, the Roman government, or a variety of different suggestions.[21] All of these suggestions have serious textual problems with them however.

We believe Cullman's proposal is the most consistent.[22] He takes note of the fact that in verse 6 the greek is neuter: *"that* which restrains." But in verse 7 it is *"he* who restrains." Why is this? He suggests that the restraining *thing* was the Divine necessity of the fulfillment of the World Mission; "the gospel must [greek dei, a divine necessity] first be published among all nations" Mark 13:10. And as the direct corollary to this, the restraining *person* was Paul, the apostle to the Gentiles.

Without question, Paul was a pivotal figure in God's eschatological scheme, 2 Timothy 4:17.[23] Thompson has noted: "He understands his mission and his call specifically as the eschatological mission to the Gentiles [Colossians 1:22-29; Ephesians 3:8; Galatians 1:16]. Indeed, he is himself the instrument of this eschatological plan [Colossians 1:24-27]."[24]

27

The Abomination of Desolation and "This Generation"

It is Paul's vital role in God's plan to bring in the Gentiles that gives insight into Romans 11:25 and the enigmatic "fullness of the Gentiles." As Thompson contends: "The 'fullness of the Gentiles' is thus the completion of Paul's missionary task." Thus, the Day of the Lord could not come per Thessalonians until Paul had completed his missionary task.

As Peter was the distinctive apostle to the Jews, Paul was the specially chosen instrument of God to the Gentiles, Acts 26:18f. Acts shows us Peter's ministry to the Jews, chapters 1-12 and then describes Paul's ministry to the Gentiles, chapters 13f. The central point of Acts is to chronicle the fulfillment of Jesus' mandate "ye shall be my witnesses in Judea, Samaria, and to the uttermost part of the earth" Acts 1:8.

The view just advanced is in harmony with the rest of Thessalonians. Paul says the restrainer would be "taken out of the way." The original language can be suggestive of a violent removal.[25] The view that the Holy Spirit is the restrainer hardly agrees with this. Yet Paul was violently removed by being martyred for his faith.

The evidence from Thessalonians and Matthew then is impressive. The Man of Sin was already active. The Restrainer was already restraining. The identity of that which restrains and the one who restrains as the World Mission and Paul, all point in the same direction--the term "this

28

The Abomination of Desolation and "This Generation"

generation" must be understood as referent to Jesus' contemporary generation.

G. R. Beasley-Murray expressed it well. After an examination of every occurrence of "this generation" he concluded that it referred to the contemporaries of Jesus. He then stated: "If dogmatic considerations were not at stake, that conclusion would not be questioned, but Biblical exegesis must control Biblical theology, not vice versa."[26] In other words, the honest Bible student must not allow preconceived ideas to control [or create!] the definition of words. He must submit to the meaning of the text; and "this generation" means Jesus' contemporaries.

CHAPTER 3

WHAT ABOUT THE END OF THE AGE?

Jesus said the gospel would be preached into all the world "then comes the end." The normal objection to the evidence just produced is: "But the end of the world did not come! Jesus did not return! Therefore, you must be wrong!" This objection is based upon a preconceived idea of the nature of the end of the age and coming of the Lord. Considering that the Jews of the first century rejected Jesus because of preconceived ideas about the nature of the kingdom, should we not at least be a little cautious here?

Unfortunately, most people believe the disciples asked Jesus about the "end of the *world*" in Matthew 24:3. This idea comes primarily from the King James translation of the Bible. But an examination of different and more modern translations, not to mention the Greek, reveals that the better translation is "end of the age."

One problem with modern interpretations is that they so often fail to properly consider the chronological context of the Biblical writings. Most people when interpreting Matthew 24:3 and the disciples' question about the end of the age assume that *the present reader* stands within *the same age* as did the disciples asking the question. But this is an assumption without merit. To properly understand the disciples' question one must realize that we live

The End of the Age

two thousand years later than they did; they lived in "this age" but you and I live in "the age to come."

It is important to understand that the Jews conceived of only two ages, "this age" and "the age to come." Biblically this is correct. The question is, what was "this age" and what was "the age to come?" To answer this we must examine some texts that speak of "this age" and "the age to come."

MATTHEW 12:32

Jesus said those blaspheming the Holy Spirit would not be forgiven "in this world, neither in the world to come." Now if the "world to come" refers to eternity after the supposed end of time it is clear that there will be sin and forgiveness in eternity. Jesus said that any sin except the blasphemy of the Spirit would be forgiven. Thus, even in the world [age] to come there would be sin and forgiveness.

If we understand Jesus' "this age" to be the Mosaic Age in which he was living and the "age to come" as the Christian Age, there is no difficulty. But if one insists that "the age to come" refers to heaven after the destruction of material creation, this demands that there be sin and forgiveness in that other dimension.

The End of the Age

MATTHEW 13:39-40

Post-millennialist Gary North calls this passage "the key continuity passage in Scripture" positing an extended future before the end of history at the parousia of Jesus. During this extended period of time the Great Commission is the mandate of the church resulting in the conversion of the nations and ultimately the Jews.[27] North continues by stating that "The Second Coming of Jesus completes the Great Commission."

The chart below will demonstrate the exact parallelism between Matthew 13 and Matthew 24. The significance of this for the postmillennialist and amillennialist cannot be overstated. Both schools believe that the Olivet Discourse refers to the events consummating in the fall of Jerusalem in A.D. 70. If therefore the relevant texts in Matthew 24 apply to the end of the Old Covenant Age in A.D. 70, then since Matthew 13 is parallel it too must apply to A.D. 70.

The End of the Age

Matthew 13	Matthew 24
end of the age, vs. 39 [suntelias ton aionion]	end of the age, vs. 3, [suntelias ton aionion]
Preaching of the gospel to all the world before the end, vs. 37-38	Preaching of the gospel to all the world before the end, vs. 14
The coming of the Son of Man, vs. 39-41	The coming of the Son of Man, vs. 29-31
The sending of the angels to gather, vs. 41	The sending of the angels to gather, vs. 31
The time of separation, vs. 40-41	The time of separation, vs. 31
Harvest is at the end of "this age" vs. 40	This generation shall not pass till all be fulfilled, vs. 34

  With this correspondence before us how is it possible to posit two different Commissions, two different "worlds," two different ends of the age, naturally resulting in two different kinds of "ages to come"; two different comings of the Lord? Since both the postmillennialists and amillennialists are almost unanimous in agreement that the passages in Matthew 24 refer to the events leading up to the coming of the Lord in A.D. 70 we find it logically impossible to deny that application for Matthew 13.

33

The End of the Age

To confirm this point, the definitive application of Matthew 13 to the end of the age in A.D. 70 is made by Daniel 12. Matthew 13:43 is a direct quote from Daniel 12:3. In that vision Daniel foresaw the coming Great Tribulation, vs. 1; the resurrection, vs. 2; the time when the righteous would shine like the stars, vs. 3; the time of the end, vs. 4; the Abomination of Desolation, vs. 9f.

In verses 6-7 Daniel overheard one angel ask another when *all*--not some, not even *most*, of these things would be fulfilled. The response was that "all these things" would be fulfilled "when the power of the holy people has been completely shattered," vs. 7. This can be no other time than the fall of Jerusalem in A.D. 70 since Jesus cites Daniel 12 no less than four times in Matthew 24 to speak of events surrounding Jerusalem's demise!

It is sad to see the lengths to which some will go to escape the force of Daniel 12. Cates for instance applies vs. 1 to the time of Antiochus Epiphanes; verse 2-3 to a yet future resurrection; verse 9f to the time of Antiochus Epiphanes.[28] This application clearly means that while the angel said *"all these things"* would be fulfilled by the time cited in verse 7 he did not *really* mean "all these things"; he only meant "some of these things!"

Second, it means *Jesus was wrong* for quoting Daniel 12:1 in his prediction of the Great Tribulation, Mat. 24:21. He was *wrong* in his application of Daniel 12:9f to the yet future, to him, Abomination of Desolation, Mat. 24:15. And it means Daniel spoke of one time of the end for these events while Jesus applied them to a totally different time of the end! It is tragic that Cates, and most other commentators, are willing to deny the Lord's application of Daniel in order to maintain their own preconceived ideas about the end of the age and the age to come! Aren't preconceived ideas what put Jesus on the Cross?

Jesus said his coming with the angels at the time of the harvest would be *"at the end of this age."* What was Jesus' "this age?" In what age was he living?

Galatians 4:4 tells us Jesus appeared in the fullness of time and was born *under the Old Law.* Hebrews 1:1 and 9:26 says Jesus appeared in the last days, at the *end of the age.* Peter specifically says that Jesus' appearance in the "last days" or "last times" referred to the days of his personal ministry and sacrifice *before Pentecost,* 1 Pet. 1:20! Since Jesus appeared in the last days and he appeared before Pentecost then undeniably, the "last days" did not begin on Pentecost! Notice the argument:

> **Major Premise**: Jesus appeared under the Old Covenant Age, Gal. 4:4.
>
> **Minor Premise**: But Jesus appeared "in the last days" 1 Pet. 1:20; Heb. 1:1.

The End of the Age

> **Conclusion**: Therefore Jesus appeared "in the last days" of the Old Covenant Age.

Jesus did not appear at *the end of time* although he appeared in the "last days" and "in the end of the age!" *He appeared in the last days of the Old Covenant World of Israel!* We concur with Wharton:

> "It is very obvious that Old Testament prophecies which are for 'the latter days,' 'the time of the end,' 'the latter times,' and 'the latter years,' are not to be interpreted as having their fulfillment in a yet future time period. They have received their fulfillment in Christ and in the church in the last days of Israel's existence, which came to an end in A.D. 70 with the destruction of Jerusalem. There are no Old Testament 'latter day' prophecies yet left of fulfillment."[29]

Matthew 13 is an Old Covenant prediction of the end of the age, vs. 43/ Dan. 12:3. As Wharton has well stated "there are no Old Testament 'latter day' predictions yet left of fulfillment." When Jesus said harvest would be "at the end of this age" Mat. 13:40, he was saying that his coming after the fulfillment of the Great Commission, would be at the end of Israel's Old Covenant Age.

The End of the Age

The fact that most people today believe we are in the "last days" is symptomatic of a tragic failure to acknowledge that the last days were in the first century. Jesus appeared in the end of the age. Peter said the events transpiring on Pentecost belonged to "the last days" as foretold by Joel, Acts 2:15f. The Old Testament prophecies do not teach that Pentecost would *initiate* the last days. They foretold events that were to occur while the last days *were already in progress*. Peter did not say the last days are *beginning*.

Paul told the Corinthians they were living in "the end of the ages" 1 Cor. 10:11. John, who predicted the coming of the "last hour" Jhn 6, also said "it is the last hour" 1 Jhn 2:18.

Upon what basis do we today insist that we are in the last days when the Biblical writers said *they* were living in the last days? Have the last days extended for two thousand years? The term "last days" denotes *a closing period of time*, and the New Testament writers insisted they were in that critical period. It is therefore anachronistic to say that the last days are still on-going.

It is important to know that the term *"end of time"* never occurs in scripture. It is always *"the time of the end."* Now it is almost universally acknowledged that Jesus

The End of the Age

appeared in the waning years of the Old Covenant World. Since this is true, why ignore that fact and insist that the New Testament writers were not speaking of their days when they spoke of the last days and the time of the end?

Why cannot the references to the "end of the age," "the last days," "the last hour," "the time of the end," "the end of all things" etc., be a reference to the consummation that was admittedly coming upon them? Why insist they were speaking of the "end of time" when it is at the same time admitted that they were living in the "time of the end" of the Old Covenant System? Are we to believe they were so unconcerned with the end of the religion, the system, *the world*, that had been and still was their very life?

Either the New Testament writers were correct [inspired!] in claiming they were in the last days or they were wrong [uninspired!]. If we are in the last days then they were wrong for they believed the last time had come and "the end of all things is at hand" 1 Pet. 4:7. But if we allow the "last days," "the end," "the end of the age," "the last hour," etc. to be referent to the last days of the Mosaic Age, then there is no such conflict. This allows us to see that when Jesus said the gospel would be preached into

The End of the Age

all the world and *then comes the end*, he was referring to the end of that Old Covenant world at the fall of Jerusalem in A.D. 70.

MATTHEW 24

There is almost unanimity among commentators that the disciples associated the fall of Jerusalem with the end of the age. Of course these same commentators claim the disciples were confused or simply mistaken. But were they? Did Jesus chide them? In Matthew 13 Jesus told several parables about the kingdom and the end of the age. He asked the disciples if they understood what he was teaching them and they responded "Yes, we understand." Did they lie? Did they lose their understanding from Matthew 13 to Matthew 24?

Jesus did not correct the disciples' understanding in Matthew 24. Since neither Matthew, Mark, or Luke give a parenthetical statement that they were mistaken in their understanding, *if it is true* that the disciples did associate the end of the age with Jesus' prediction of the judgment of Israel then we have no alternative but to accept this as the definition of the end of the age!

Further, the parallel between the Olivet Discourse and Revelation lends full credence to the view that the end of the age occurred with the judgment of Jerusalem.

The End of the Age

Matthew 24	Revelation 14
Great Commission, v. 14	Great Commission, v. 6
Judgment on Jerusalem, v. 15f	Judgment on Babylon, v. 8
Coming of the Lord, v. 29f	Coming of the Lord, vs. 14f
Gathering of the elect, v. 30-31	Gathering of the elect, v. 13
This generation shall not pass until all be fulfilled, v. 34	The hour of his judgment has come, v. 7

The significant thing for both the amillennialist and postmillennialist is that both schools agree that each of the texts cited from Matthew 24 refer exclusively to Christ's coming in A.D. 70. But since Matthew 24 refers to that event and time then patently Revelation does as well.[30] While many postmillennialists have no problem with this implication many amillennialists do. The premillennialist rejects both of these ideas and protracts these events into our imminent future. In doing so he violates the chronological limitations Jesus placed on his prediction: "this generation shall not pass."

The End of the Age

The parallel between the texts is very obvious. The only thing that would need to be established would be the identity of Babylon. If Babylon is Jerusalem of the first century then the Great Commission, the end of the age, and Christ's coming would be demonstrated to be linked not with an end of time but with the A.D. 70 parousia of Jesus. We would present just a tiny fraction of the evidence that Babylon was indeed first century Jerusalem.

1.] Unless one can prove positively that the New Testament teaches about two Great Commissions related to the end of two different ages at two different kinds of comings of Christ then the evidence is suggestive that there was only one New Testament eschatology. That deals with Christ's coming against Jerusalem.

2.] Babylon persecuted "the prophets," Rev. 16. This term, when appearing without qualifiers, signifies exclusively Old Covenant prophets.[31] Jesus identified Jerusalem as the city guilty of persecuting

Old Testament prophets, Mt. 23:29f; Luke 13:31f.

3.] Babylon had filled the cup of her sin by persecuting the prophets, saints, and followers of Jesus, Rev. 18:20, 24. Jesus said it was first century Jerusalem that would fill her cup of sin because she had killed the prophets and would kill the ones he sent to her, Mat. 23:29f.

4.] The judgment on Babylon would finish the wrath of God, Rev. 15:8. But Jesus said that in the fall of Jerusalem "these be the days of vengeance when all things that are written must be fulfilled" Luke 21:22.

5.] Jesus said the martyrs of God, all the way back to creation, would be judged in his coming against Jerusalem, Mat. 23:31-39. Revelation depicts the vindication of the martyrs of God at the judgment of Babylon, 16:4-6, 17-21; 18:20-24.

These are but a few of the abundant pieces of evidence that substantiate the claim that Babylon of Revelation was first century Jerusalem.[32]

Now since the disciples associated the fall of Jerusalem with the end of the age and Jesus did not correct them, this is evidence that the end of the age was indeed A.D. 70. Further, the correlation of Revelation 14 and Matthew 24 confirms this identification. The end of the age is not a reference to the end of time but to the end of the Old Covenant Age of Israel.

MARK 10:30

Jesus told his disciples that "in the age to come" believers would receive "eternal life." Notice the contrast between "now in this time" and "the age to come."

For Jesus, eternal life and the age to come were inextricably linked. This is because under the Old Covenant Age there was no eternal life, Gal. 3:20-21; Heb. 10:1-4. But in 1 John 5:10-13 the inspired apostle wrote: "this is the record, that God has given us eternal life"; "he that has the Son has life; he that does not have the Son of God has not life"; "these things I write unto you that you may know that you have eternal life."

The End of the Age

Since eternal life would be in "the age to come," and since John said his brethren were recipients of eternal life, it follows that the "age to come" had already broken in. This is shown by reading 1 John 2:8: "the darkness is passing away, and the true light is already shining." For the New Testament writers, "the light" and "the Day" were all terms associated with the "Age to Come." Darkness was associated with "this age" or the "present evil age" Gal. 1:4.

Not only did John believe that the age to come had broken in, he believed he was living in the closing critical period of "this age." He said: "the darkness" i.e. the Old World, *is passing away*." Notice he did not say the darkness had already passed away! It was passing away! In 2:17-18 he said "the world is [present tense!] passing away"; "little children, it is the last hour: as you have heard that antichrist should come, even now there are many antichrists, whereby we know that it is the last hour."

Now if John was saying *the end of time* and *material creation* had arrived, he was plainly wrong. But when we see that John was anticipating the end of the Old Covenant World of Israel as predicted by Jesus, since the fall of Jerusalem was within a few short years of John's writing the

The End of the Age

passage makes perfect sense.³³ This means that John envisioned himself living during a transitional period between the Old World and the New; between "this age" and the "age to come." The New Age had dawned, the Old Age was passing.

Since John was one of the ones who asked Jesus about the sign of the end of the age and heard his prediction about the preaching of the gospel to all the world before the end, we think it too much to ask to divorce John's declaration about the imminent end from that context. John plainly has Jesus' prediction about the end of the age in mind. But since the end of the age in Matthew 24 must refer to the end of the Old Covenant World of Israel then this must be what John is alluding to as well.

LUKE 20:27-37

In this passage the Sadducees attempted to entrap Jesus with a question about the resurrection. The Sadducees thought Jesus affirmed a physical resurrection as did the Pharisees. But Jesus denounced their assumptions showing that the resurrection is a spiritual reality. A full discussion of this passage is not possible in this small work.³⁴ Our chief concern is with the idea of "the age to come."

The End of the Age

The Sadducees presented the case of a woman married to seven men through the Levirate marriage tradition. The Levirate marriage system was an intergal part of the Old Covenant World and one of the means by which the nation was maintained. It is difficult to overestimate the importance of the Levirate marriage law to Israel. The Mosaic World truly was nurtured and sustained by "marrying and giving in marriage" since it was a nation dependent upon purity of bloodline. As King says "Israelite marrying and giving in marriage had a distinctive meaning and purpose that set it apart from common, ordinary marriage in other nations."[35]

Jesus debunked the Sadducees by contrasting the "this age" practice of "marrying and giving in marriage" with "that age," the age of the resurrection, in which there would be no marrying and giving in marriage. The key question is, what age followed the age in which the Levirate marriage was practiced? Jesus said "the sons of *this age*, marry and are given in marriage." This referred, not to the general practice of mankind in general, but to the Levirate marriage law that is the focus of the discussion. Thus, what age was to follow that in which the Levirate marriage was practiced? That is quite simple: it is the New

The End of the Age

Covenant Age of Jesus Christ. This can be shown by a closer examination of Luke 20. Jesus said that in the age to come, the resurrection age, 1.] there would be no marrying; 2.] those of that age would not die; 3.] the resurrection would make them sons of God, vs. 36. Do these conditions exist today in Christ? Yes, indeed.

In Galatians 3:28 Paul told his readers that if they were in Christ, they were *"neither male or female."* Now if one is neither "male or female" it is a little difficult to be married, is it not? Thus, in Galatians 3 we find the very thing predicted by Jesus as a reality in Christ.

Patently, Paul is speaking of the spiritual world of Christ in Galatians. He was contrasting the world of Christ with the Old Covenant World of Israel in which blessings were dependent upon physical lineage associated with Abraham. It was dependent upon "marrying and giving in marriage!" But the apostle says that now in Christ the blessings of Abraham belong to those born of the Spirit, not of the flesh, cf. Gal. 4:22-32 and John 3:1f.

In Luke 20 Jesus also said that those in the resurrection "age to come" could never die since they would be equal to the angels, vs. 36. Do those in Christ today die?

The End of the Age

Physically they do of course. But this is not the issue.

Jesus said "if anyone keeps my word he shall never see death" John 8:51; he said "my sheep hear my voice...and I give them eternal life, and they shall never perish" John 10:27-28; "whoever lives and believes in me shall never die" John 11:26. It is undeniable that if Jesus was speaking of physical death in these passages that no person has ever been a Christian since every person since he uttered those words has died physically! The Jews believed Jesus *was* speaking of physical death, John 8:52f. They were like so many today who focus on the physical and not the spiritual. But Jesus was not speaking of physical death; he was speaking of a *relationship*, of spiritual life!

In Galatians 3:26-29 Paul told the brethren they had become *children of God* by faith when they were baptized into Christ. It cannot go unnoticed that the same writer likened baptism to *resurrection*, Rom. 6:3-4! Remember, in Luke 20 Jesus said those in the age to come would become *sons of God by means of the resurrection*.

Now if "that age" has not come, do we not have a right to wonder if there are any Sons of God today? Did not Jesus say the resurrection would make those of that age sons of God? Therefore, if "that age" has not come then no one today can be a Son of God!

Herein is further proof that Jesus was contrasting Covenant Ages and not the physical world as opposed to a yet future existence after the supposed end of time. Under the Old Covenant "sons of God" were produced by "marrying and giving in marriage," i.e. by natural procreation into a Covenant relationship with God. But under the New Covenant men are "born again," Jhn 1:11-12; 3:3f; they become children of God by faith, Gal. 3:26. Under the New Covenant men are *taught then born*, whereas under the Old Covenant they were *born then taught*, cf. Hebrews 8.

According to Jesus then, those who come into him *are neither male nor female; they never die*; they become *the sons of God* by dying and being raised in baptism! Every element of the resurrection age, the "age to come," is present in Christ's New Covenant World!

When Jesus uttered his prediction in Luke 20, his "this age," the Old Covenant World, had not yet passed. He had said that World could not pass until the Old Covenant was *completely fulfilled*, Mat. 5:17-18. In Luke 21, the sermon that deals with the coming *end of the age*, Mat. 24:2-3, he said in the fall of Jerusalem "all things that

The End of the Age

are written must be fulfilled." He said that would occur *in that generation* after the gospel had been preached to all the world for a witness to the nations, Mark 13:10, 30. The end of the age occurred with the fall of Jerusalem in A.D. 70!

The End of the Age

The Consummation of the Age:
A Closer Look

That the end of the age was related to the passing of the Old Covenant World of Israel and not the end of time is demonstrated by a closer examination of the term "end of the age." We have already seen that this is a distinctive greek term "suntelias tou aionos." This term appears a total of six times in scripture. Every occurrence can be shown to be related to the end of Israel's Theocracy in A.D. 70.

1.] Matthew 13:39, 40, 49-- See the discussion above. To briefly reiterate, Matthew 13:43 is a direct quote of Daniel 12:3. In that chapter predicting the "time of the end" Daniel overheard one angel ask another when the things foretold would be. The response was "when the power of the Holy People has been completely shattered all these things will be fulfilled." Now since Matthew 13 quotes Daniel 12, and since Daniel 12 would be fulfilled when the power of the Holy People would be completely shattered, and since the power of the Holy People was completely shattered in A.D. 70 then the time of the end, the "end of the age" [suntelia tou aionos] occurred in A.D. 70.

2.] Matthew 24:3--The disciples asked about the sign of the end of the age [*suntelias tou aionos*]. Jesus said the gospel would be preached into "all the world then comes the end." As we have seen the gospel was preached into all the world in that generation before the fall of Jerusalem.

Second, it cannot be ignored that the Olivet Discourse contains no less than four direct allusions or quotes of Daniel 12: about the time of the end, 12:4/24:3; about the Great Tribulation, 12:1/24:21; about the Abomination of Desolation, 12:11/24:15; about the time for the fulfillment of all things, 12:7/Luke 21:22.

Daniel 12 foretold the time when Israel would be completely destroyed and the Olivet Discourse predicted the final overthrow of Israel's Theocratic relationship. Daniel foretold the time of the end; Matthew predicted the end of the age [suntelias tou aionos]. How is it possible to maintain that Jesus foretold a different time of the end than did Daniel?

3.] Matthew 28:20--Jesus promised his disciples that as they went preaching the gospel to all the world--in fulfillment of his earlier prediction, Mat. 24:14--he would be *with them* "to the end of the age" [*suntelias tou aionos*]. This promise to be "with them" was the promise of the miraculous gifts of the Spirit to inspire, empower, and confirm them in their mission, Mk. 13:9f. The testimony of scripture is that "they went out and preached everywhere, the Lord working with them, and confirming the word through the accompanying signs" Mk. 16:20. See also Acts 14:3; Heb. 2:1-4, etc. Now if the end of the age of Matthew 28 has not yet come then the disciples of Jesus should have the gifts of the Spirit such as inspiration, tongues, prophesy, etc. Yet the Biblical record is clear that those gifts were to end in the first century at the Day of the Lord, Acts 2:17-22; 1 Cor. 1:4-8, etc.. If the gifts of the Spirit have ceased then the end of the age of Matthew 28 has come!

The End of the Age

>4.] Hebrews 9:26--Jesus appeared in *the end of the age* [*suntelias ton aionon*]. Jesus did not appear at the end of time. He *did appear* in the final generation of Old Covenant time however! Time was running out on that Old World, Heb. 8:13! Jesus was born under the Old Law, Gal. 4:4, and as seen above, it is widely admitted that he appeared in the waning years of the Old Covenant System. Why not give this fact full force in our understanding of "the end of the age?"

The term "end of the world" was used primarily by Matthew as a quick glance above reveals. Would it not be unusual for a writer to use such a distinctive and unusual term in such dramatically different ways as suggested by most commentators today?

It is evident from this brief study that the greek term *suntelias tou aionos* is not a common term in the New Testament and that it is applied to the end of the Old Covenant World of Israel. There is no way to divorce the identical term as used in Matthew 13 from its usage in Matthew 24 or chapter 28, or Hebrews 9. The direct association of the term as found in Matthew 13 with Matthew 24 and in turn Daniel 12 is prima facia evidence for identifying the end

The End of the Age

of the age as the time of Israel's demise in A.D. 70. This means but one thing: the end of the Age occurred in A.D. 70. This agrees perfectly with Jesus' prediction that the gospel would be preached into all the world "then comes the end."

We cannot examine every passage that mentions "this age" and "the age to come." But these are some of the pivotal texts to help us define those terms. We have seen that when Jesus predicted the preaching of the gospel into all the world before *the end of the age*, he was not referring to the end of the material world, or the end of the Christian Age. The Christian Age has *no end*, Luke 1:32-34; Eph. 3:20-21! Jesus was referring to the end of the age in which he was living--the Old Covenant World of Israel.

CHAPTER 4

THE WORLD MISSION AND
THE END OF THE LAW

Many people believe the Mosaic Age ended at the Cross. They insist that the Old Law was nailed to the Cross and that the New Covenant Age began on Pentecost.

The Old Law passed *by the power of the Cross* but not at the time of the Cross! Those coming into Christ were *dying to the Law*, Rom. 7:4, but the Law was in the process of growing old and was ready to pass away years after the Cross, 2 Cor. 3:6-18, Heb. 8:13. See our work on Matthew 5:17-18 for a fuller discussion of this issue.[36]

Jesus appeared in the last days, Heb. 1:1. But Jesus appeared *before Pentecost*. Therefore the last days did not begin on Pentecost as many claim. Since Jesus appeared in the last days and he appeared before Pentecost this demands that the last days must refer to the last days of the Mosaic Age!

The Old Covenant Age could not have ended at the Cross for a very simple reason. Jesus appeared in the "end of the age" [sunteleia ton aionon], Heb. 9:26. In Matthew 24:3 the disciples asked him when the "end of the age" [sunteleias tou aionos]

The World Mission and the End of the Old Law

would occur. He said *the gospel must be preached into all the world before the end could come*, Mat. 24:14! If the Mosaic Age ended at the Cross, the gospel must have been proclaimed into all the world before the Cross! Yet the gospel did not even began to be proclaimed until Pentecost-- after the Cross!

Further, after the Cross Jesus was still anticipating the end of the age, [sunteleias tou aionos], Mat. 28:19! And he was anticipating it in direct association with the World Mission as he predicted in Matthew 24. Since Jesus, *after the Cross*, was still anticipating the end of the age, the end of the age did not come at the Cross!

Now since *"the age to come"* would **fully** come after the *"end of the age"* and since the end of the age refers to the Mosaic Age, it is apparent that the disciples in Matthew 24 were not inquiring about the end of time but the end of the Old World of Israel! This is the only context that satisfies Jesus' prediction that the gospel would be preached into all the world in that generation and then the end would come. The gospel was preached into all the world. The end of the age came in the destruction of Jerusalem.

The World Mission and the End of the Old Law

Further confirmation that the "end of the age" was the Old Covenant Age of Israel is to be found in the fact that Jesus said the Old Covenant, i.e. the Law of Moses could not pass until it was all fulfilled, Matthew 5:17-18:

> "Think not that I am come to destroy the Law and the Prophets: I am not come to destroy but to fulfill. For verily I say to you that until heaven and earth pass, one jot or one tittle shall in no wise pass from the Law until all be fulfilled."

It is unfortunate that the tradition in which this author was raised completely distorts Jesus' words. Jesus said *none* of the Law would pass *until all* was fulfilled; the amillennial view says *all* of the Law would pass *when some* of it was fulfilled! There is something tragically wrong with a theology that must radically alter and distort the words of scripture to sustain itself.

The amillennialist appeals to Luke 18:31-33. Jesus was to fulfill all that was written concerning him. The point is made that Jesus used the term "all" in reference to the fulfillment of the Law and Prophets. Since all he mentioned was his passion then

The World Mission and the End of the Old Law

that was all that was necessary for the passing of the Law.

But Luke 18 does not mention the passing of the Law! Second, Jesus very clearly limits the meaning of "all" in the text by specifically referring to his passion. In other words, the "all" under view is specifically defined by Jesus. He was not speaking of all that was necessary for the passing of the Law. He was speaking of the fulfillment of all things relating to his passion! The text in Matthew 5 is comprehensive; Luke 18 is specific! It is a gross misuse of scripture to limit Matthew 5 based upon Luke 18. This assumes that no other text may speak of other things that would also be necessary for the complete fulfillment of other aspects of the Law! Unfortunately, theological necessity is the mother of forced interpretations.

Jesus said all of the Old Law had to be fulfilled before it could pass. The question is: Did the Old Covenant predict the World Commission? And the answer is unequivocally, "Yes!" Read Luke 24:44-47:

> "And he said to them, These are the words that I spake unto you, while I was yet with you, that all things must be fulfilled, which are written in the Law of Moses, and in the Prophets, and in the Psalms

The World Mission and the End of the Old Law

concerning me. Then he
opened their understanding,
that they might understand
the scriptures. And he said to
them, Thus it is written, and
thus it behooved the Christ to
suffer, and to rise from the
dead the third day: and that
repentance and remission of
sins should be preached in his
name among all nations,
beginning at Jerusalem."

✶ Jesus said all things foretold in the Law and Prophets had to be fulfilled and he said this included the preaching of the Gospel to all nations! The Old Law predicted the completion of the World Mission, e.g. Isaiah 11:9.

Please note that Jesus reminded his disciples of the time when he told them that all of the Old Testament had to be fulfilled-- this was in Matthew 5:17-18! Since Jesus was reminding them of Matthew 5 and since that context certainly discussed the necessity for the fulfillment of all the Law for it to pass, then of necessity Luke 24 is discussing the necessity of the fulfillment of all things *for the passing of the Law*.

While there was more that Jesus could have listed from the Old Testament that needed to be fulfilled, he listed only

The World Mission and the End of the Old Law

three things in Luke 24. But *two of these three things extended beyond the Cross*! Thus, since he said all had to be fulfilled before the Law could pass and since what had to be fulfilled extended beyond the Cross then the Law extended beyond the Cross.

The three things necessary for the fulfillment of "all things" were 1.] His death; 2.] His resurrection; 3.] that repentance and remission of sins should be preached to all the nations beginning at Jerusalem. Take specific note of number three--the World Commission. Jesus said for all of the Law, the Psalms and the Prophets to be fulfilled *the gospel had to be preached to all the world*!

Some contend that since there were devout Jews, proselytes and believers *from every nation* present on Pentecost, Acts 2, and since the gospel was preached to them that day, that in a representative sense the gospel was preached to all the world that day. This will not do for several reasons.

First, the preaching of the gospel foretold in Luke 24 included preaching to all the nations, i.e. *it included the Gentiles*. The word translated nations is "ethnos"; it is translated "nations" 61 times, "Gentiles" 93 times; "heathens," 4 times, and "people," two times.[37] Only 11 times does the word "ethnos" refer to the Jewish nation. In each of these texts the word has a modifier such

The World Mission and the End of the Old Law

as "this nation," "my nation" etc., that demands the identity of the Jewish nation. The word "ethnos" normally signifies the Gentiles.

Paul confirms this in Acts 26:22-23. On trial before Agrippa he defends his ministry. He taught "none other things than those which the prophets and Moses did say should come. That Christ should suffer, and that he should rise from the dead, and should shew light unto the people, and to the Gentiles." Paul is all but quoting from Luke 24. He says his ministry to the Gentiles was foretold by Moses and the prophets.

Thus, in Luke 24 Jesus said all things written in the Law of Moses had to be fulfilled. He said that included the proclamation of the Gospel to all the world. This included the Gentile nations and this was not accomplished on Pentecost.

Another reason why Pentecost cannot be the fulfillment of Luke 24:47 is based upon the greek text. Jesus said the Gospel would be preached "among all nations" KJV. The word rendered "among" is "eis" and better means "into" or "to." "To" all the nations is the more common translation. This might seem insignificant at first but the next greek word is very significant.

Jesus said the Gospel would be preached into all the world "beginning from

The World Mission and the End of the Old Law

Jerusalem." The word "from" is from the word "ek" and means away from. The force of the word is that *beginning at Jerusalem and going out from there* the Gospel would be preached *to all the world*. Plainly, Pentecost did not fulfill of Luke 24:47.

Our argument in regard to the preaching of the Gospel and the passing of the Old Law and the End of the Age is this:

> **Major Premise**: All of the Old Testament had to be fulfilled before the Old Testament could pass, Mat. 5:17-18.
>
> **Minor Premise**: But the preaching of the Gospel into all the world was foretold by the Old Testament, Luke 24:44-47; Acts 26:22-23.
>
> **Conclusion**: Therefore the Gospel had to be preached into all the world before the Old Testament could pass.

In light of this, Matthew 24:14 is easily understood. Jesus said the Gospel had to be preached into all the world "then comes the end." The end he was speaking of

The World Mission and the End of the Old Law

was the Old Covenant World of Israel. The preaching of the Gospel into all the world was foretold by Israel's prophets, cf. Isaiah 11:9. As a promise to Israel these salvation promises were "irrevocable" Romans 11:28-29--they had to be fulfilled! This brings us to briefly consider a vital issue: the fulfillment of Israel's promises.

The millennialist holds that the proclamation of the gospel is *in one sense* unrelated to the eschatological scheme. It is true that millennialists see the fulfillment of the World Mission as a sign of the end. At the same time however, since the gospel is the proclamation of the establishment of the church and salvation to the Gentiles the World Mission is part and parcel of *a failed mission by Jesus*! The millennialist holds that Jesus came to establish the kingdom for Israel, the Jews rejected him, therefore the church was established to preach the gospel to the world.[38] But the New Testament is emphatic: the preaching of the gospel was the proclamation of the fulfillment, not the failure of Israel's promises!

In Acts 2 Peter declared that Jesus had become, not given the right to become, Lord and Christ; he is on David's throne as promised, verses 16-36. In chapter 3 Peter stated that God, in fulfillment of the promises to Abraham had sent Jesus, vs. 24f.

The World Mission and the End of the Old Law

The prophets had foretold "these days," that was the *first century*, not the twentieth!

In Acts 7 Stephen said that Jesus was the present, not future fulfillment of God's promise to send a savior. In chapter 13 Paul expounded: "we declare unto you glad tidings-that promise which was made to the fathers. God has fulfilled this for us their children in that He has raised up Jesus." Acts 15 teaches that in fulfillment of Amos 9:11 God had raised again the "tent" of David. The proof of this is the conversion of the Gentiles. Amos said God would restore the tent of David so that Gentiles could come in; the Gentiles were coming in, therefore God had fulfilled [and was fulfilling!] his promises to Israel!

The entire Roman epistle, but especially chapters 8-11, is Paul's dissertation on God's faithfulness to Israel. He said God had not cast off Israel, 11:1. He said that while "Israel has not obtained that for which she sought" nonetheless "the remnant has obtained it" 11:7. The remnant had and was realizing the fulfillment of God's promises to Israel! If God's promises to Israel were nationalistic and the remnant had received the fulfillment of that promise then the remnant had received nationalistic restoration! But it is clear those promises

The World Mission and the End of the Old Law

were being fulfilled spiritually in Christ *in the church*, not a nationalistic revival!

This is the context of Paul's statement that the gospel had been preached into all the world, 10:13-18. God was faithful to His promises to Israel and had declared that faithfulness by sending the gospel to all the world "to the Jew first, then the Greek."

Further, God was *still being*, and *would be* faithful to Israel: "all Israel shall be saved" 11:26. [Here is the already but not yet concept of salvation and eschatology! The "not yet" fulfillment of God's promises to Israel was to be of the same nature as the "already." The already was *salvation in Christ*, not national revival and restoration.] And this was so because God's promises to Israel were "irrevocable" 11:29. The millennialist fails to see that Paul is not projecting a future restoration of national Israel but the perfection of Israel's messianic hopes in Christ at the parousia, vs. 26. But again, the key is Paul's message was one of fulfillment, not postponement.

The significance of this message--the gospel as the fulfillment of God's promises to Israel, also strikes at the very foundation of the amillennial view.

Romans 11:26-27 is a reiteration of God's Old Covenant prediction to bring

The World Mission and the End of the Old Law

salvation to Israel. Specifically, Romans 11:26-27 is a quote of Isaiah 27; 59:20-21, and Jeremiah 31. The amillennial view is that all of God's covenant promises to Israel were fulfilled at the Cross and his Covenant relationship with her terminated there.[39]

Paul said God's promise to save Israel was "irrevocable" Rom. 11:29. In other words, God had to fulfill his Covenant promises to Israel! This is simply another way of saying "until heaven and earth pass away, not one jot or one tittle shall pass from the law until all is fulfilled" Matthew 5:17-18. Israel could not pass as God's Covenant people until God had completely fulfilled his Covenant promises to Israel. Yet in Romans 11:26 Paul is citing Old Covenant promises made to Israel and says those promises were yet to be fulfilled!

Major Premise: The Old Covenant and God's Covenant relationship with Israel could not pass until all Old Covenant promises were fulfilled. Romans 11:29; Matthew 5:17-18.

Minor Premise: But the Old Covenant promise of Israel's salvation was still valid in Romans 11:26-29.

The World Mission and the End of the Old Law

> **Conclusion**: Therefore the Old Covenant and God's Covenant relationship with Israel was still valid in Romans 11:26-29.

To emphasize this point please ask yourself this question: If a law or covenant has been abrogated or annulled, are any of its promises or penalties applicable anymore? The answer is so simple and clear that no thinking person would challenge it: an annulled covenant is just that--*annulled*!

If God's Covenant with Israel was annulled at the Cross, why was Paul in 55-59 A.D. still anticipating the fulfillment of God's Old Covenant promises Israel? If God had already fulfilled his promises to Israel then Israel had already received her salvation! If God's *covenant relationship* with Israel had been annulled then how could Paul say that God's *covenant promises* to her were still valid? The fact that Paul in Romans 11:26f was still anticipating the fulfillment of Israel's Old Covenant promises is *prima facia* proof that the Old Covenant did not pass at the Cross.

Combined with our study above, of the end of the age, the significance of the completion of the World Mission and the passing of the Old Law is fully revealed. The

The World Mission and the End of the Old Law

ideas dovetail perfectly. Israel's Age would end only when Israel's Covenant was fulfilled. But Israel's Covenant would be finally and fully fulfilled at the fall of Jerusalem after the preaching of the Gospel into all the world, Mat. 24:14; Lk. 21:22. The fall of Jerusalem, the end of the age and the passing of the Law are inextricably linked.

The city of Jerusalem was a Covenant City. When she had peace she knew there was peace between her and her God, Ps. 41:10-12. But her own scriptures foretold a time when that Covenant relationship would come to a full end, Daniel 9:24-27.[40] A New Everlasting Covenant of Peace would be established, Is. 51; Jer. 31; Ezek. 37.

As the substance and "good stuff" of a walnut is not the external shell but the inner body, the substance of God's promises lay not in the external polity of Israel but in the spiritual. The Old National Israel would find her fulfillment in the New Spiritual Israel. But the Old had to be laid aside and destroyed as a definitive sign that God truly was finished with the Old. The Old could not be laid aside until it had fully exhausted its purpose and found total fulfillment.

The completion of the World Commission not only involved the fulfillment of Old Testament scriptures, it was the

The World Mission and the End of the Old Law

proclamation and offer of Israel's anticipated kingdom. Thus, the necessity of the extension of the Gospel "to the Jew first and then to the Greek."

God could not reject Israel until Israel had rejected this offer, Acts 13:46. Or to put it another way, God could not reject Israel until Israel had rejected God. This is shown in Galatians 4:22f.

In his famous allegory Paul said that just as Ishmael, the son of the flesh, persecuted the son of the promise, Isaac, "as it was then, even so it is now." It is imperative to see that it was Paul's "now" not ours! The children of the promise were the first century Christians; the "children of the flesh" was first century Israel. The Jews were persecuting the children of the promise--the spiritual seed of Abraham, Galatians 3:26-29! And what did Paul say was about to happen? "Cast out the bondwoman and her son!"; Israel was to be cast out for persecuting the church!

The amillennialist says God was through with Israel at the Cross. But this would mean, per Galatians 4, that the church was in existence and had been persecuted by Israel before the Cross! Paul said Israel would be cast out for persecuting the church!

The World Mission and the End of the Old Law

The persecution of the Christians was a direct result of the on-going fulfillment of Jesus' mandate to preach the gospel to the world. As the church proclaimed the fulfillment of *Israel's promises in Christ* they went first of all to the Jews. Even Paul the apostle to the Gentiles went to the Jew first.

The preaching of the Gospel therefore was both a declaration of God's faithfulness to Israel in establishing the kingdom, and it was a declaration of the impending dissolution of the Old Kingdom that had fulfilled its purpose and was now "ready to vanish away" Heb. 8:13. This preaching led to rejection by those intent on maintaining the Old Ways and persecution of those bringing this message of transformation. This dual message of establishment and dissolution was the message of fulfillment of Israel's promises. And complete fulfillment was the ultimate prerequisite for final dissolution.

CHAPTER 5

THE WORLD MISSION, MIRACLES, AND THE END OF THE AGE

Not only was the passing of the Old Law linked with the fulfillment of the World Mission, but the miraculous work of the Spirit was limited to the "last days" and coupled with the completion of the World Mission.

Space forbids a lengthy discussion of the miraculous work of the Spirit. A few facts however, are very clear from scripture.

1.] The *time for the outpouring of the Spirit* was "in the last days" Joel 2:28/ Acts 2:15f.

2.] The *nature of the outpouring of the Spirit* was miraculous--"your sons and your daughters shall prophesy," Joel 2:28f.

3.] The *purpose of the outpouring of the Spirit* was to empower the church to fulfill the World Commission, Luke 24:48-49; John 14-16; Acts 1:4-8. In Mark 13, when Jesus predicted the World Commission he told his disciples that when they were persecuted for proclaiming his word they would be divinely empowered to defend it.

4.] The *termination of the outpouring of the Spirit* was to be the Coming of the

The World Mission, Miracles, and the End of the Age

Lord, Mat. 28:20; John 14:16-18; Acts 2:17, 20; 1 Cor. 1:4-8.

While there were other reasons for the outpouring of the Spirit, i.e. revelation and confirmation of the truth, Mk. 16:20; to serve as a Comforter for the apostles in the absence of Christ, John 14:16; to bring about "the unity of the faith" i.e. Jew and Gentile equality, Rom. 15:14-21; Eph. 4,[41] there is *no doubt* that Jesus said the miraculous work of the Spirit would empower the church for her task of World Mission, Acts 1:4-8. [Note: The other functions of the Spirit were directly related to the World Mission!]

Jesus' words are clear: "you shall receive power...and ye shall be my witnesses." Therefore, if Jesus' original mandate is unfulfilled and the Spirit is still present as promised, then the church should without doubt possess the miraculous empowering gifts of the Spirit!

In promising his disciples the empowering gift of the Spirit Jesus was harkening back to the prophet Joel. In that Great promise of God's actions for the last days the outpouring of the Spirit lies at the center of focus. And a proper understanding of Joel's promise is absolutely vital to understanding Biblical pneumatology and eschatology.

The World Mission, Miracles, and the End of the Age

> The prophecy of Joel 2 stands as the foundation for all New Testament pneumatology.

As Camp says, the prophecy of Joel 2:28f "gives the commencement, characteristics, and consummation of miraculous gifts."[42] Joel's prophecy stands as the foundation of all New Testament pneumatology. *It is imperative to see the eschatological significance of the gift of the Holy Spirit as it related to the World Mission.*

THE HOLY SPIRIT AND ESCHATOLOGY

Francis comments: "The manifestation of the Spirit at Pentecost was an eschatological event, and one connected with the climactic cosmic drama."[43] He is surely correct in seeing the inextricable connection between the outpouring of the Spirit and eschatology.

When on Pentecost Peter cited Joel 2:28f he did not alter the original prophecy into a paradigm for world history--an extended "time between" before the consummation. He said *"this is that."* He did not say "this is similar, but different." Does it not behoove the student to accept Peter?

Joel said the Spirit would be poured out before the Great and Notable Day of the Lord. As we shall see the "day of the Lord" is a common OT concept for an "in-time" judgment coming.

Peter tells his audience that upon obedience they too can partake of Joel's promise, vs. 38-39. He then exhorts them "Save yourselves from this perverse generation" vs. 40. Peter clearly has a sense of imminence in mind when he said "save yourselves from this perverse generation."

The outpouring of the Holy Spirit was an eschatological sign--it was the sign of an event that *did occur in that generation.* As Bales asks: "The wonders of Acts 2:17-18 took place in that generation, why not the destruction which was implied in the day of the Lord in verses 19-20?"[44] Peter did not dissociate the day of the Lord from the outpouring of the Spirit--he cited the OT prophecy linking the outpouring of the Spirit as a sign of that Day. He said that prophecy was being fulfilled. He urged his listeners to save themselves from that generation. How much more of an association between the Spirit and the Parousia could he have made?

It is difficult for this scribe to understand the belief that those miraculously endowed individuals were *mistaken about the time of the end!* If one admits that the Holy Spirit was poured out in miraculous measure

> The Sign of the last days was the outpouring of Joel 2 and the day of the Lord was the end of the Sign.

in the first century, and the Spirit inspired individuals to speak and write, then how is it possible that those inspired writers and preachers were *wrong* in their insistence that the Lord's coming was near? If the outpouring of the Spirit was miraculous the eschatological element inherent in, and the predictions of its imminence, were inspired.

The *first century imminence* of the Parousia belies the modern concept of imminence. Something *truly imminent* in the first century cannot be imminent today! If the outpouring of the Spirit was an eschatological sign--and that is indisputable-- then there must have been a direct temporal link between the sign and the event it signified. As Mattill says "How unlikely for an apocalyptist to split up the end events so that the signs of the end occur in his generation but the end itself is to arrive at a lengthy interval thereafter, perhaps hundreds or thousands of years later."[45]

Hoekema, among others, agrees that the outpouring of the Spirit on Pentecost "had great eschatological significance."[46] But to him the entire Christian Age is the "last days" period. This view destroys the relationship between sign and event.

Further, this view *demands* that if we today have the gift of the Spirit as promised by Joel--there *must be miracles, including*

The World Mission, Miracles, and the End of the Age

tongues, today![47] Joel's prophecy contains no element of the "non miraculous." This presents significant problems for those who believe the gifts of the Spirit have ceased.

Ladd for instance argues that the outpouring of the Spirit was "an eschatological event belonging to the day when God finally redeems his people Israel, and gathers them into his Kingdom. It is therefore associated with the Day of the Lord, which will be both a day of judgment and of salvation [Joel 2:30-32]."[48] He also says we today have the Spirit present. Yet he insists the charismata associated with that outpouring are not present.

You cannot maintain the presence of the Holy Spirit without implying of necessity the presence of miraculous gifts and the imminence of the end!

If the outpouring of the Spirit, evidenced by the miraculous, was an eschatological *sign of the end*, and if we today no longer have the miraculous gifts of the Spirit, then does this not indicate that "the Great and Terrible Day of the Lord," [Acts 2:20], has come?

The World Mission, Miracles, and the End of the Age

TONGUES ARE FOR A SIGN!

As we have just seen, the New Testament definitely posits the charismata as signs of the end. The apostle Paul, in 1 Corinthians 14:21-22, cites Isaiah 28:11f and says "Tongues are for a sign."

Isaiah was announcing impending judgment on Israel at the hands of the Assyrians. This judgment was the fulfillment of Covenant Wrath predicted in Deuteronomy 28:49: "The Lord will bring a nation against you from afar, from the end of the earth, as the eagle swoops down, a nation whose language you shall not understand." Jeremiah 5:15 also cited Deuteronomy to announce judgment at the hands of Babylon in B. C. 586.

Is it not significant that Paul cites Isaiah 28? As Robertson has noted: "It is not that Paul simply snatches up an isolated aphorism to apply to his circumstance. He knew full well that tongues in Isaiah appeared as a sign of covenantal curse. He understood that judgment on Israel was the subject at hand. In short, Paul quoted Isaiah 28:11 precisely because he understood the New Testament phenomenon of tongues to be a climactic fulfillment of Old Testament prophecy."[49]

The World Mission, Miracles, and the End of the Age

Once again, the miraculous gifts of the Spirit were a sign of impending judgment. Historically tongues [although not miraculous] were one of the signs to Israel of Covenantal judgment. As Robertson continues: "The judgment of God on Israel in 586 B.C. was only a foretaste of that severest of judgments pronounced by Christ himself: 'Your house is left to you desolate.' Luke 13:35'"

Since Paul taught that he was living in the end of the age and that the end was imminent, does not his reference to tongues as a sign give us a direct link to the nature of the end he was anticipating? Chilton has correctly stated the case: "The miracle of Pentecost was a shocking message to Israel. They knew what this meant. It was the sign from God that the Chief Cornerstone had come, and that Israel had rejected Him to its own condemnation [Mat. 21:42-44; 1 Pet. 2:6-8]. It was the sign of judgment and reprobation, the signal that the apostates of Jerusalem were about to 'stumble backward, be broken, snared and taken captive.' The Last Days of Israel had come: the old age was at an end, and Jerusalem would be swept away in a new flood, to make way for God's New Creation. As Paul said, tongues was 'for a sign, not to those who believe, but to the unbelievers' [1 Cor. 14:22]--a sign to the unbelieving Jews of their approaching doom."[50]

Those today who would make tongues a sign of the "end of time" are without Biblical evidence and support. That doctrine stands outside of the Covenantal framework of the miraculous and tongues in particular. Tongues were a sign of the end of the Old Covenant World of Israel.

THE HOLY SPIRIT AND WORLD MISSION

When Jesus commissioned his disciples to go into all the world he *empowered* them. This empowerment was nothing less than the miraculous power of the Holy Spirit: "But when they arrest you and deliver you up, do not worry beforehand, or premeditate what you will speak. But whatever is given you in that hour, speak; for it is not you who speak but the Holy Spirit" Mk. 13:11.

Gary North has correctly noted: "The sending of the Holy Spirit was the empowering of the Great Commission."[51]

Notice just a few references in Acts in regard to the mission and miraculous work of the Spirit.

1.] Acts 3:1-26--miraculous healing leading to preaching.

The World Mission, Miracles, and the End of the Age

2.] Acts 4:30-31--outpouring of the Spirit; "and they spoke the word of God with all boldness."

3.] Acts 5--"many signs and wonders were done among the people"; and many believers were added to the Lord, vs. 12-14.

4.] Acts 8--Philip went to Samaria and "preached Christ to them," vs. 5. "The multitudes with one accord heeded the things spoken by Philip, hearing and seeing the miracles he did" vs. 6.

5.] Acts 10--Peter was instructed, against his wishes, to preach to the Gentiles. It took a miraculous manifestation to convince him to go, [10:9f], and a miraculous outpouring to convince him further that the Gentiles could indeed be equal participants in the kingdom, vs. 44-48.

The mystery explained

6.] Acts 13:6ff--When Paul preached the gospel he was confronted with opposition from Bar-Jesus, Paul miraculously strikes him blind and "the proconsul believed" vs. 11-12. As Jesus promised: *preaching, persecution, power*. [More on this later!]

7.] Acts 14:1f--We find here the *preaching* of the gospel, with *power*, vs. 3--"signs and wonders" were done by Paul and Barnabas; and *persecution*, vs. 2, 5.

The evidence is indisputable--the work of the Spirit in empowering the church to fulfill the Great Commission was miraculous. The implication is clear therefore: if the Great Commission has not been fulfilled and if the Spirit is still present then *there must be miracles today!*

This has serious implications for the non-charismatic[52] who insists the Commission has never been fulfilled and yet the Spirit is present. Where are the miracles if the Great Commission has not been fulfilled? If we are in the last days characterized by the outpouring of the Spirit, since that outpouring definitely involved the

The World Mission, Miracles, and the End of the Age

prophetic office and inspiration, [1 Cor. 13; Eph. 4], then we must today still have the prophetic office and inspired men!

The non-charismatic wishes to maintain the first century *character* of the Commission while denying the first century *power* of the Commission!

But the charismatic has an equal or greater problem. He must face the facts: **1.]** The inspired apostles emphatically stated that they were in the last days. **2.]** They stated the end was imminent in their lifetime, James 5:7-9; 1 Pet. 4:7. **3.]** They stated that the people then living would live and possess the miracles until the day of the Lord, 1 Cor. 1:4-8. **4.]** Related to #2, the direct relationship between the miraculous signs and the imminent end. The signs were first century phenomenon. The end must have been in the first century. **5.]** The empirical reality that the so-called miracles of today are not true miracles when compared to those of the Biblical account.

In summary then we must recognize certain facts about the relationship between the Spirit and the Mission:

    1.] The presence of the miraculous was a *sign* of the imminent coming of the Day of the Lord.

The World Mission, Miracles, and the End of the Age

2.] Jesus gave the miraculous
gifts to empower the church
for her World Mission.

3.] Jesus promised that he
through the miraculous Spirit
would be with the church
until the "end of the age"
John 14:16-18; Mat. 28:20.

4.] The mission was fulfilled
in the first century.

Since Jesus promised to empower the church for her mission by means of the miraculous Spirit until the end of the age, and since the first century church fulfilled the World Mission, we believe the end must have come in the first century. After all did Jesus not say "into all the world, then comes the end"?

CHAPTER 6

WHAT ABOUT
THE COMING OF THE LORD?

It will be objected that while the New Testament writers were anticipating the imminent coming of the Lord, it never occurred. The Lord did not come as predicted, therefore we should simply ignore those time statements of imminence and live today *as if* Jesus was coming soon. But this view creates a tremendous problem, and ignores Biblical testimony.

First, to admit that Jesus predicted his coming for that generation but insist it did not occur impugns Jesus' inspiration. The test of a prophet was whether his predictions came true, Deut. 18:18f. Thus, if Jesus indicated a soon return and did not fulfill his prediction he is a false prophet.

There can be no doubt that Jesus predicted his return for his generation. In Matthew 10:22-23 he told his disciples that they would not have gone throughout all of the cities of Israel in fleeing from the coming persecution, before he would come. In Matthew 16:27-28 he told his audience that there were some standing there that would not taste of death until they saw his coming in judgment and glory. Now either

Defining the Parousia

some of those people are still alive, he lied, he failed, or he came.[53] Many other passages say Christ's coming was imminent in the first century, see Rev. 22:6, 10, 12, 20.

Most Bible students are sadly unfamiliar with the true meaning of "coming of the Lord" language. The western mind-set tends to take literally such language as coming on the clouds, with angels, with the sound of a trumpet and a shout, the destruction of "heaven and earth," etc.. With a little more care in research however, it would be easily determined that this language was never used to describe a literal coming of the Lord and the destruction of literal creation.

Isaiah 13:10 describes the destruction of "heaven and earth." Taken literally this would be a prophecy of material creation. But verse one reveals this was a prophecy against ancient Babylon. Verse 17 says the Medes and Persians would accomplish the destruction. In Daniel 5 the Medes destroyed Babylon. Thus, the language of the passing of heaven and earth was a figurative description of the passing of Babylon's "world."

Isaiah 19 says Jehovah would ride a cloud into Egypt to destroy that country; chapter 20 names the Assyrian king that

Defining the Parousia

accomplished that destruction. God "came" by means of the Assyrian ruler.

When Jehovah destroyed the Assyrians it was predicted that he would come "burning with His anger"; he would come with a shout and in flaming fire. This was not fulfilled literally, but when the Lord destroyed 185,000 of the Assyrians in one night as they besieged Jerusalem, their world came crashing down around their ears! See Isaiah 30; 37.

Isaiah 34 graphically describes the dissolution of earth and the heavens passing away. Yet verse 5-6 says this was a prediction of the fall of the Edomites. Babylon destroyed Edom in 583 B.C.. Edom's *world* ended but physical creation was not destroyed.

When describing the impending captivity of Israel, Micah said: "The Lord will come out of his place; he will come down and tread on the high places of the earth" Micah 1:3-4. The Assyrians carried Israel captive in 721 B.C.. God never literally came out of heaven and earth never actually melted. But Israel's world was destroyed. Thus, the Lord "came" in the fall of Babylon, Assyria, Israel, Jerusalem, etc..

Every single constituent element associated with the predictions of the Lord's parousia in the New Testament find their origin in the Old Testament. The coming on the clouds, Isa. 19, with a shout, Ps. 18, with the angels, Deut. 33; Is. 13, in flaming fire, Is. 30, the destruction of "heaven and earth" Is. 13, 34, etc. This language is without exception figurative. Should we interpret it literally just because it is in the New Testament books?[54] In the New Testament the pattern is no different for two reasons.

First, the New Testament writers were trained in the Old Testament and familiar with this figurative use of language. Indeed, as Minear says: "As one recalls Old Testament passages like these, [Joel, Isaiah, etc, DKP] one is forced to conclude that every essential feature in the New Testament prophecies was an echo of these. No Christian prophet tried to explain the meaning of these references to solar disasters, a fact that suggests that the audience was expected to understand the language. The vocabulary was fully indigenous to the community in which the prophet functioned. Modern readers, therefore, must compare this idiom not with modern views of the cosmos but with an ancient outlook within which an intelligible message was conveyed without undue difficulty."[55]

Second, the New Testament writers specifically say they are quoting Old Testament prophecies in regard to the

Defining the Parousia

passing of "heaven and earth" 2 Pet. 3:1-2. Since the consistent Old Testament pattern was to describe the fall of a nation in terms of the destruction of creation at the coming of the Lord from heaven on the clouds, and since Peter says his prediction of the passing of the heaven and earth at the day of the Lord is simply a reiteration of Old Testament predictions, upon what basis does one interpret 2 Peter 3 literally? How does the New Testament interpreter change or ignore the consistent use of language established by Old Testament precedent and pattern? If the New Testament writers changed the consistently spiritual use of language to literal, should we not find some firm evidence of this? The New Testament writers often do reveal the *spiritual significance* of Old Testament language, e.g. the nature of the kingdom. But *never* do they apply Old Testament figurative language literally.

Some seek to delineate between what they admit to be the spiritual coming of Christ in A. D. 70 and a yet future event. Cates for instance properly observes that the language of the Lord's coming in Matthew 24:29f is typical Old Covenant language to describe God's actions in judgment.[56]

Defining the Parousia

He then seeks to show that Jesus' "real" coming must be different because...well, because he says so! But he gives very little evidence and what is offered is untenable. He says the future coming will be different, [i.e. literal and bodily] because, Jesus will actually leave heaven but concerning the Old Covenant comings he says, "Which of these times did God leave Heaven to carry out His will? Not one of them!" Had he read the scriptures a little closer he would never have made such an unfortunate statement!

In Isaiah 31:4 it speaks of God's "coming" to deliver Jerusalem from the Assyrians: "the Lord of Hosts will come down." In Micah 1:3 it says in reference to the time when God punished Israel for her sins by means of the Assyrians: "the Lord is coming out of His place; He will come down." The point is that, as stated above, every constituent element of eschatology finds its source in the Old Testament. In the Old Covenant the Lord "came out of heaven"; not bodily or literally, but He came nonetheless. And this is precisely the language Jesus used to speak of his coming.

When he spoke of his coming on the clouds with power and great glory, Jesus was not using literal language. He was, in the

Defining the Parousia

established manner of Israel's prophets, using hyperbole to describe the coming judgment on Israel. And in light of the consistent figurative application of the passing of heaven and earth to the destruction of a nation, we can better understand that when Jesus said "heaven and earth will pass" Mat. 24:35, he was responding to the disciples' questions about *the destruction of Jerusalem*, Mat. 24:2. The focus was on the *world of Israel*, not on material creation.

      What needs to be understood is that the New Testament record was written to convince that "Jesus is the Christ the Son of the living God" John 20:30-31--**to establish the true deity of Jesus**. With the deity of Jesus established the predictions of his "coming" are to be understood in the same light as the coming of Jehovah in the Old Covenant. This is precisely what we see when Jesus was on trial before Caiaphas. The High Priest asked him if he was the Christ and he answered: "It is as you said. Nevertheless, I say to you hereafter you will see the Son of Man sitting at the right hand of the Power, and coming on the clouds of heaven." Caiaphas' immediate reaction was "He has spoken blasphemy!"

Defining the Parousia

The High Priest well understood that Jesus was claiming the Sovereign prerogative of Deity! Jesus' statement about "coming on the clouds" was referent to the majesty of Jehovah, Psalms 104; the exercise of judgment, see the references above; and the reign of Messiah, Daniel 7:13-14. The reference to his coming had nothing whatsoever to do with cumulus clouds or a literal coming; it had everything to do with Jesus' identity as the Divine Son of God!

Jesus, and the New Testament writers were living in the closing period of the Old Covenant World. They constantly emphasized the imminence of that coming consummation: "the end of all things is at hand" 1 Peter 4:7; "the time has come for the judgment to begin" 1 Pet. 4:17; "the coming of the Lord is at hand" James 5:8; "in a very little while the one who is coming will come and will not tarry" Hebrews 10:37; "it is the last hour," 1 John 2:18.

To those who would honor the inspiration of scriptures the reality of this language of imminence demands a spiritual interpretation of Jesus' promise to return in his generation. Whereas it can be easily demonstrated that language of the coming of the Lord and the destruction of heaven and earth is consistently metaphoric, time

Defining the Parousia

language is most often not metaphoric.
Thus, the consistent use of metaphoric
language to describe the parousia leads us to
interpret Jesus' predictions in this way.
Further, the language of imminence
demands it if we would maintain a high view
of Jesus and his Word.

CHAPTER 7

THE PREACHING AND THE END: A CLOSER LOOK

Our premise is this: since Jesus predicted the preaching of the gospel into all the world before the end, and since "the end" must refer to the Old Covenant World of Israel, then those passages that link the preaching of the gospel and the parousia [coming of the Lord] must be based upon Jesus' foundational prediction. We hold that the New Testament writers constantly had Jesus' prediction in mind. As events unfolded they were reminded of the prediction and their writings reflect this.

In what follows we propose to show that New Testament passages normally used to support a yet future coming of Christ at the end of time must refer instead to the end of the Old World of Israel. Paul especially mentioned the proclamation of the gospel in light of the coming parousia and end of the age.

Preaching, Persecution, Power, Parousia!

Romans 9-13

In Romans 10:16-18 the apostle asserted in no uncertain terms that the gospel had been proclaimed into all the world. See the chart above. Did Paul also see the coming of the Lord as imminent in light of this accomplished fact? Yes indeed.

In chapter 9:28 Paul cited the promise of God to bring redemption to Israel. That promise was that when God began his work of saving the remnant "he will finish the work and cut it short in righteousness, because the Lord will make a short work upon the earth." Now that promised salvation would be fully revealed at the coming of the Lord, Rom. 11:26-27. The salvation of Israel *had begun*, Rom. 11:7f. God had promised it would be perfected shortly at the coming of the Lord. The coming of the Lord would only occur at the end of the age after the gospel had been preached into all the world. But the gospel had been preached into all the world. Therefore the coming of the Lord must have been imminent. And Paul says it was.

In Romans 13:11-12 the Cilician apostle says: "knowing the time that now it is high time to awake out of sleep; for now our salvation is nearer than when we first believed. The night is far spent, the day is at hand." In chapter 16:20 the same writer said

95

Preaching, Persecution, Power, Parousia!

"And the God of peace shall crush Satan under your feet shortly."

    This last verse, 16:20, is set directly within the context in which Paul once again affirms the completion of the Great Commission. In verse 26 he declares that the gospel had been "made known to all nations for the obedience of faith"; a direct allusion to Matthew 28:18. How can we ignore or deny the connection in Paul's thought between the completion of the Commission and the imminent end?

    Very clearly Paul, after saying the gospel had been preached into all the world, asserts that the Day of the Lord was imminent, the Day of Salvation was shortly to come. It is evident that Jesus' prediction is the foundation for Paul's writing. Since Jesus associated the preaching of the gospel and the end of the Old Covenant World, and since Paul emphasized the *fulfillment* of the Commission and proclaimed the *imminence of the end*, the end in view must be the Old Covenant World of Israel at the fall of Jerusalem in A.D. 70.

Preaching, Persecution, Power, Parousia!

1 Corinthians

The same writer who in Romans said the gospel had been proclaimed into all the world says the Corinthians would possess the gifts of the Spirit until the Day of the Lord, 1 Cor. 1:4-8. In chapter 7:29-31 he said "the time has been shortened" [cf. Mat. 24:22]. In verse 31 he said "the fashion of this world is passing away." In chapter 10 he asserted that they were living in the end of the age, vs. 11. In 15:50f he stated that not all of the Corinthians would die before the coming of the Lord. Chapter 16 closes with the urgent prayer "Maranatha, O Lord Come!" vs. 22.

One simply cannot divorce these references to the impending end from the fact that the gospel had been preached into all the world.

There is a fourfold pattern in the Olivet Discourse that then runs throughout almost every New Testament book: *preaching, persecution, power, parousia*. Simply put Jesus said the gospel would be *preached* into all the world, Mark 13:10. They would also be *persecuted* as they preached, Mark 13:9-10. But they would be miraculously endowed with the gifts of the Spirit [*power*] as they went proclaiming that gospel, Mark 13:11. And Jesus promised to

Preaching, Persecution, Power, Parousia!

come [*parousia*] in glory, vindication, and victory, Mark 13:26f. And he promised to come in that generation, Mark 13:30.

This pattern is in Corinthians. The *preaching* is the focus in chapters 1-2. The *persecution* is present in many texts, e.g., 4:12f. The *power* is also present in 1:4-8; 2:1-4. The *parousia* promise is ubiquitous as seen above.

The fourfold pattern in Mark relates to the proclamation of the gospel prior to the coming of the Lord at the end of the Old World of Israel. Since the pattern is identical in Corinthians we conclude that the parousia promise of Corinthians relates not to an end of time but to the end of the Old Covenant World of Israel.

Philippians

The Philippian church had supported Paul's efforts to spread the gospel [*preaching*] to all the world, 1:5, 7. He and they had suffered *persecution* for their faith, 1:28. It was through the *power* of the Spirit that Paul expected to finish his mission, 1:19. But Paul was "eagerly waiting" [apekdekomai] for the *parousia* and confident that "the Lord is at hand" [parousia] 3:20; 4:5.

Since the pattern in Philippians is the identical pattern as in the Olivet Discourse,

Preaching, Persecution, Power, Parousia!

and that in the Olivet Discourse clearly relates to the end of the age parousia of Jesus in the fall of Jerusalem, how can we say that Paul is dealing with another, different coming of the Lord at a different end of the age?

It is significant that the amillennialist believes that Matthew 24:4-35 relate to the fall of Jerusalem.[57] This means that the pattern of *preaching, persecution, power, parousia* relates to the A.D. 70 coming of Jesus. But the recognition that this pattern *permeates the epistles* brings home the harmony of the New Testament and causes us to realize that the fall of Jerusalem was the event the writers had in mind and not some supposed end of time.

If the pattern of Matthew 24:4-35 relates to the A.D. 70 coming of Jesus, and the epistles contain the identical pattern, then one can hardly say the pattern in the epistles refers to a different coming! The failure to appreciate the significance of the fall of Jerusalem is one of the major failings of the modern church.

Colossians

In Colossians 1:5-7 inspiration declares that the gospel had been proclaimed in all the world [kosmos], exactly

Powerful Parallels!

as Jesus predicted, Mk. 16:15. In verse 23 the apostle said the gospel had been preached to every creature [ktisis] under heaven; just as Jesus commanded that the gospel be preached to every creature [ktisis], Mk. 16:15. The Commission was fulfilled!

Not only had the Commission been fulfilled, [*preaching*], the Colossians and Paul, were recipients of the *power* of the Spirit, 1:11, 29, even though they, with Paul, suffered *persecution*, 1:24. But their hope was the soon to occur coming of Christ, [*parousia*], Col. 3:1-3.

Given Paul's intense emphasis on the completion of the Commission, the power of the Spirit and persecution, how can one divorce his epistle from the fourfold blueprint pattern of the Olivet Discourse? And if that is the pattern behind Colossians it follows that the parousia of Colossians 3 must refer to the A.D. 70 coming of Christ to bring redemption and the kingdom to perfection, Luke 21:26-32.

1 Thessalonians

The parousia of Jesus is the theme that permeates the Thessalonian epistles. What is often overlooked is that Thessalonians is a direct echo of the Olivet Discourse.[58] The fourfold pattern of the Discourse runs throughout the epistles.

Powerful Parallels!

In 1:1:5f Paul said the gospel had been proclaimed by the Thessalonians throughout the Macedonian region and beyond, yea, *"in every place"* vs. 7. The Thessalonians were fulfilling Jesus' mandate to preach the gospel into all the world before the end! That *proclamation* of the gospel by Paul to the Thessalonians and then by them was attended by the miraculous *power* of the Spirit, 1:5. And the apostle was quick to observe that the Thessalonians had been converted to "wait for His Son from heaven" [*parousia*] 1:10, even as they were being *persecuted* for their faith, 1:2:15f.

The direct parallelism between the Olivet Discourse and Thessalonians is established beyond doubt by a comparison between Matthew 24:29-31 and 1 Thessalonians 4:13-18. The chart will help visualize the comparison.

Powerful Parallels!

Matthew 24	Thessalonians 4
Coming of the Lord, 31	Coming of the Lord, 15
with the angels, vs. 30	with the angels, 16
with the clouds, vs. 30	with the clouds, 17
with the Trumpet, vs. 31	with the Trumpet, vs. 16
to gather the elect, vs. 31	to gather the elect, vs. 17
This generation shall not pass till all these things be fulfilled, vs. 34	Those of us who are alive and remain until the coming of the Lord, vs. 15, 17

In Thessalonians Paul says he is only reminding his readers of what the Lord had already said "this I say to you by the word of the Lord" 4:15. What is so important about this is that *the only passage* from Jesus' ministry containing *every constituent element* listed by Paul in Thessalonians is the Olivet Discourse! Thus, whatever Matthew 24 is describing, Thessalonians is describing! But Matthew 24 is a figurative description of the coming of the Lord in judgment at the end of the Old Covenant World of Israel in A.D. 70. Therefore Thessalonians is a figurative description of the same event!

Powerful Parallels!

The fourfold pattern of *preaching, persecution, power, parousia*, is the same in the Olivet Discourse and Thessalonians. The description of the Day of the Lord is the same in the Discourse and Thessalonians. Since the *pattern* is the same, since the *description* is the same, and since *the time statements* are the same, we conclude that the passages must be speaking of the same time and event; the A.D. 70 coming of the Lord.

The proclamation of the gospel into all the world is something ever before Paul's eyes. Equally significant to him was the impending parousia. The reason for this connection is to be found in the Olivet Discourse. For Paul and the early church the completion of the World Mission was a sure sign that Christ's "second coming" was truly at hand. The confident assertion that the mission had been completed gives added validity therefore to the repeated declarations that "in a very little while, he who is coming will come and will not tarry" Heb. 10:37.

Today's Bible student must either accept as inspired the declarations of the completion of the Commission and therefore the true imminence of the parousia in the first century, or he must be willing to deny

Powerful Parallels!

these inspired statements and extend the end into a future far removed from the inspired writers.

Titus

"The grace of God that brings salvation, has appeared to all men" said the apostle Paul in Titus 2:11. Was Paul mistaken? Was he deluded with visions of grandeur? Or was he fully cognizant of Jesus' Olivet prediction and declaring its fulfillment? Any view that denies a relationship between Jesus' prediction and Paul's declaration may be guilty of prejudice and blindness brought on by traditionalism!

Not only did the apostle say the gospel had been declared to all men, he said they were *expecting* the Savior, vs. 13! When he said they were "looking for the blessed hope and glorious appearing of our Great God" he used a word "prosdekomai" that better means "expecting."

Why would Paul say the gospel had been preached to every man and therefore they were *expecting* the Savior's coming? Because Jesus said "the gospel will be preached into all the world and then comes the end!" Paul's expectation was based upon the fulfillment of Jesus' prediction!

Powerful Parallels!

Unless one can establish beyond doubt that Paul's statements about the fulfillment of the Commission were false, or were unrelated to Jesus' prediction, then the association between prediction and fulfillment is established. Since the "end" that was to follow the preaching of the gospel into all the world has been shown to be the coming of Jesus at the fall of Jerusalem in A.D. 70 we must conclude that Titus speaks of that event.

1 Peter

Peter's epistle fairly bristles with expectation of the coming of the Lord. And his epistle also clearly reflects the fourfold pattern of the Olivet Discourse.

In 1 Peter 1 the apostle of Jesus speaks of the *preaching* of the gospel by the *power of the Holy Spirit*, vs. 12. His readers were being *persecuted*, vs. 6-7, but were anticipating the *revelation of the Lord* after they had suffered "a little while" vs. 6-7.

Peter's expectation of the consummation cannot be extended into the far future by any honest student of scripture. He said salvation was "ready to be revealed in the last time" vs. 5--and he was living in the last time, vs. 20. He confidently affirmed that Jesus was then "ready to judge the living

Powerful Parallels!

and the dead" 4:5, because "the end of all things is at hand" 4:7; and "the time has come for the judgment to begin at the house of God" 4:17.

Significantly, when he refers to "the time" he uses both the definite article and a word for "time" [*kairos*] that means "appointed time." In addition he says "*the* judgment." Peter was affirming that the appointed time for "the judgment" had arrived, compare Acts 17:30-31! These were not merely "we *hope* it is at hand" or "*it could be* at hand" statements. These are divinely inspired declarations that the appointed time of the end was near!

The preaching of the gospel into all the world plainly lies behind this epistle since Peter is addressing "the pilgrims of the dispersion in Pontus, Galatia, Cappadocia, Asia, and Bithynia." The implication of such a widely dispersed audience is clear, the gospel message was everywhere!

Was Peter unaware of Jesus' prediction that the gospel would be preached into all the world and then the end? Certainly not; he was on the Mount and heard Jesus' prediction, Mark 13:3. How then can we divorce Peter's epistle from that context since he deals with the same pattern? When Peter, aware of Paul's epistles wherein he declared the fulfillment of the Commission, 2 Pet. 3:16, said the end was at hand, how do we envision a different end than that predicted by Jesus? Why should we resist such harmony in scripture to hold onto traditional concepts?

1 John

We have already seen that for Jesus eternal life was inextricably linked with the "age to come"; and that 1 John states that eternal life was being given in Christ. Further proof that the age to come had broken in and that the end of the age was imminent is to be found in the fact that the four-fold pattern of Olivet is also in 1 John.
John reminds his readers of the declaration of the gospel [*preaching*] to his readers, 1 Jhn. 1:3. The brethren to whom he writes were *empowered* by the miraculous "anointing" of the Spirit: "you have no need that anyone teach you"; just as Jesus had promised in Mark 13:9f. The apostle reminded his readers that they should not be surprised when the world hated them [*persecution*] because this was exactly what the Lord had foretold, 3:13. Compare Mark 13:13; John 15:18f; 16:1-4. But they were to abide faithful until the *parousia*, 2:28, even

Powerful Parallels!

as the anointing of the Spirit would abide with them, 2:27.

John, like Peter, was on the Mount of Olives when Jesus gave his prediction containing the fourfold pattern. Should we discount and ignore the direct harmony and parallel nature of what Jesus predicted and what John said was happening around him and his readers? Jesus said those things were to occur in his generation. John, still living in that generation, wrote that those things were happening. Does this not force us to acknowledge the temporal and contemporary force of "this generation" in Matthew 24:34?

The presence of the fourfold pattern as predicted by Jesus coupled with John's emphatic and urgent declaration "it is the last hour!" should cause the honest Bible student to reexamine his concepts about the end of the age and the coming of the Lord.

Since the fourfold pattern of the Olivet Discourse relates exclusively to the coming of the Lord at the end of the Old Covenant Age in A.D. 70, and since 1 John reveals the identical pattern, this demands that we see that "the last hour" and the "world is passing away" are references to the consummation of the Old Aeon of Israel.

Powerful Parallels!

Jude

Jude was convinced he was in *the last days*, vs. 17, [was he wrong?] and experiencing the very things foretold by the prophets of old and the apostles. He stated that the gospel had been once for all delivered [*preaching*] to the saints, vs. 3. He urged his readers to pray in the Holy Spirit [*power*], as they were "looking for the mercy of our Lord Jesus Christ" [*parousia*] vs. 20. This "looking" is from the same word found in Titus 2, see above. His reference to "looking for the mercy of the Lord" is a technical term for looking for [expecting!] the coming of the Lord.

In Jude we find the identical pattern revealed by Jesus on the Mount. The preaching of the gospel into all the world was a definitive sign of the impending end of the age. Like Paul and Peter, Jude said the gospel had been delivered and they were expecting the parousia because they were living in the last days foretold by the apostles.

How does one deny this imminence without doing grave insult to inspiration? How does one insist the gospel has never been preached into all the world without accusing the Bible writers of naivete, delusion, over exuberance, or falsification?

Powerful Parallels!

Revelation

John's apocalypse contains the identical emphasis on the preaching of the gospel into all the world prior to the end as does the Olivet Discourse. In fact, it could be argued that while John's gospel does not contain a record of the Discourse, his Apocalypse is the "long version" of what the other gospels recorded. The fourfold pattern of *preaching, persecution, power, parousia* appears not once but at least twice in this book, in chapters 11 and 14. The chart will help visualize the comparison with the Olivet Discourse.

Powerful Parallels!

Olivet Discourse	Revelation 11, 14
Preaching to all nations, Mark 13:10	*Preaching*: 11-two witnesses; 14:6-everlasting gospel to preach to all nations
Persecution, Mark 13:9-10	*Persecution*: Two witnesses slain, 11:7-8
Power, Mark 13:11	*Power*, witnesses have power to call down fire from heaven, 11:5-6
Parousia, 13:26-Son of Man on the Clouds of Heaven	*Parousia*, 11:15f; 14:14f-Son of Man on Clouds of Heaven
This Generation, 13:30	The Hour of His Judgment has come, 14:7; no more delay in fulfillment, 10:7
Against Jerusalem, 13:1-4	Against city where the Lord was slain, 11:8

In Revelation 14 John saw an angel with the everlasting gospel fly through heaven. His mission was to *preach* that gospel to "every nation, and kindred, and tongue and tribe" verse 6. That message was: "The hour of his judgment is come!" The judgment was on the Great city of Babylon

Powerful Parallels!

for *persecuting* the saints and prophets. This city is first century Jerusalem for it is the city "where the Lord was crucified" 11:8.[59] In verses 14f we find the coming of the Lord [*parousia*] in judgment.

This pattern is perhaps even more graphic and specific in chapter 11. We find the two witnesses whose task it is to proclaim God's message, [*preaching*]. They are miraculously endowed with *power*, vs. 5-6. When they finish their task they are slain, [*persecution*], vs. 7. They are then resurrected [*parousia*] at the time of the judgment on the city where their Lord was crucified, 11:8, 11f.

The parallels between the Olivet Discourse and Revelation are too obvious and too precise to ignore. Jesus said the gospel would be *preached* into all the world by the Spirit endowed [*power*] church undergoing *persecution*, and promised his *parousia* to give the victory and kingdom, in that generation. He said that judgment would be against Jerusalem.

The amillennialist and postmillennialist generally agree that the passages from the Discourse apply only to the events culminating in the coming of the Lord against Jerusalem. This being the case, how is it possible to deny that application of the Apocalypse when every constituent element of the Discourse is found not once but twice in Revelation? And how does the

Powerful Parallels!

premillennialist deny the first century application of these events without denying the emphatic statements of scripture?

Before leaving Revelation, we think it apropos to examine it in light of a text examined earlier, Matthew 13. The parallelism between Revelation 14 and Matthew is precise.

Matthew 13	Revelation 14
Proclamation of the Word, [implicit] vs. 37-38	Proclamation of the Word, 14:6
Coming of the Son of Man, 13:41	Coming of the Son of Man, vs. 14
Sending forth of Angels, vs. 41	Sending forth of Angels, vs. 14f
Time of the harvest, 39-40	Time of the harvest, 16-19
Righteous shine, 43	Righteous blessed, 13
Harvest is at the end of "this age" vs. 39-40.	The time of his judgment has come, vs. 7.

As we have seen, Revelation deals with the judgment of Old Covenant Israel and Babylon, Jerusalem her capital. The agreement with Matthew 13 is powerful.

Powerful Parallels!

Two bits of converging evidence show that the two texts must apply to A.D. 70.

We have seen that Matthew 13:43 is a direct quote from Daniel 12:3 and Daniel 12:7 says the fulfillment of that prophecy would be when the power of the holy people was completely shattered--this was A.D. 70. Thus, Matthew 13 is A.D. 70. But Matthew 13 is parallel to Revelation 14. Therefore, Revelation 14 was predictive of A.D. 70.

Second, Revelation 14 was the prediction of Babylon's judgment. But the judgment of Babylon was the judgment of Jerusalem. Matthew 13 and Revelation 14 are parallel. Therefore, Matthew 13 predicted the end of the age in A.D. 70. These two pieces of evidence amount to a *prima facia* demonstration of our construct.

The implication of this comparison for the postmillennialist is great. Chilton for example applies Matthew 13 to "the end of the world."[60] On the other hand, in his tome on Revelation Chilton says chapter 14 applied to the preaching of the gospel into all the world before A.D. 70.[61] This is inconsistent. Where is the exegetical support for this? Is the desire to maintain a futurist eschatology so strong that exegetes are willing to ignore such powerful evidence?

Now since both Matthew and Revelation deal with the same thing, judgment on Israel at the end of her Old

Powerful Parallels!

Covenant Age, then the significance and relationship of the Great Commission to that event is firmly established.

Since Matthew and Revelation are identical the harmony and unity of Biblical eschatology is also confirmed. The New Testament is not a record of many "end of the ages"; not many "end of the worlds"; not many "last days" or "last hours." The New Testament writers anticipated one consummation, one end of the age. The writers did not anticipate the end of a Covenant Age, then the end of time. They did not eagerly await a spiritual return of Christ on the clouds then a literal coming of Christ on clouds. In the fulfillment of the Great Commission they preached *"the* parousia"; *"the* end of *the* age" *"the* end of all things" The pattern of *preaching, persecution, power, and parousia* that permeates the entirety of the New Testament manifests this in a forceful way.

The Great Commission had incredible eschatological significance. But it did not herald nor signify the end of time. The Great Commission and its first century fulfillment must be seen within the context of God's Covenant dealings with his people.

What we see from this overview then is that the pattern of *preaching, persecution,*

Powerful Parallels!

power, and parousia, truly does permeate the New Testament corpus. It is in each of the synoptic gospels. It is in John, especially chapters 14-16: *preaching,* 14:27; *persecution*, 16:1-2; *power*, 14:26; 15:26; *parousia*, 14:1-3.

The pattern is in Acts: *preaching*, 1:8; *persecution*, not specifically in chapter 1 but accompanies the preaching throughout Acts; *power*, 1:8; *parousia*, 1:11. Philemon may be the only New Testament book that does not manifest this pattern!

Jesus' mandate, prediction, and pattern in Matthew 24 is the definitive teaching that underlies the rest of the New Testament doctrine about the end. But we have shown that his predictions of the end related not to some supposed end of time but the end of the Old World of Israel. This was in A.D. 70 with the fall of Jerusalem.

The recognition and acknowledgment of Jesus' fourfold pattern binds the New Testament together into a wonderful unity. It avoids the pitfalls of denying the relationship of the World Mission and eschatology. It honors the emphatic time statements about the time of the end. It honors the Biblical writer's insistence that the Commission had indeed been fulfilled. It eliminates the need to create two vastly different kinds of "the end of the age," comings of the Lord, New Creations, resurrections, etc.. It honors the Covenantal nature of eschatology.

The mention in so many epistles of the completion of the Commission is not just coincidental, braggadocio, or delusion. The inspired writers were reminding their readers of Jesus' prediction, its fulfillment, and therefore of the impending parousia.

We find then the very clear, though challenging, teaching that the end of the age and coming of the Lord was to occur in the first century and was associated with the fall of Jerusalem in A.D. 70. To deny that was the end of the age one must:

1.] Deny that the gospel was preached into all the world as the apostle Paul and others said it had.

2.] Deny that the "last days" existed in the first century and instead extend that period over two thousand years. But to do this is to deny the inspired writer's testimony that they were indeed living in the last days.

3.] Deny that the Abomination of Desolation occurred in the first century as Jesus predicted. Yet Jesus told the church in Jerusalem what to do when they saw the Abomination, and we know that at the outset of the Jewish War the early church did what Jesus commanded.

4.] Deny the consistent usage of the distinctive greek term "suntelias tou aionos" and make the term mean two totally different things even though it is used primarily by the same author in the same book in the same kind of contexts, i.e. in contexts dealing with the coming of the Lord and evangelism.

5.] Deny the meaning of "this generation" since Jesus said the end of the age, the preaching of the gospel to all nations, the Abomination and his coming were to all occur in his generation, Mat. 24:34. Yet we have seen that one cannot change the meaning of "this generation" without doing harm to inspiration.

6.] Ignore the eschatological significance of John the Immerser as Elijah; deny his message of imminent judgment; ignore the significance of his appearance in the first century.

7.] Deny the very clear parallelism between the Olivet Discourse and the rest of the New Testament in regard to the *preaching, persecution, power, and parousia*. The parallels are too clear to deny. Since the pattern established in Matthew relates to the proclamation of the gospel prior to the end of the Old Covenant World of Israel, and since the epistles contain the identical pattern, then the epistles must be speaking of the same end of the age.

While preconceived ideas are challenged by the fact that Jesus predicted

Powerful Parallels!

all these things to occur in his generation, and challenged by the fact that history and inspiration record *that they happened*, the honest Bible student must come to grips with the Biblical testimony.

CHAPTER 8

Implications of Fulfillment

The implications of the first century fulfillment of the Great Commission are devastating to the traditional views of eschatology. It means the **millennialist** is wrong because the dispensational view says that the proclamation of the gospel, although a sign of the end, is unrelated to the fulfillment of Israel's promises.[62] It says the church age is an interim measure unforeseen by the prophets and primarily "the time of the Gentiles." But as we have shown, the proclamation of the Gospel was the proclamation of *the fulfillment*, not the *postponement* of Israel's promises.

The millennialist is wrong to say the gospel has never been preached into all the world. It means he is wrong when he says we must be living in the last days since the gospel is being preached as never before. It means he is wrong to say because of this preaching that the coming of the Lord is at hand and must be in this generation.

One of the pillars of millennialism is the belief that our generation is the one to preach the gospel into all the world. But this pillar is defective because it denies the inspired testimony! The gospel was preached

What Does All This Mean?

into all the world in the first century--the end came in the first century.

Postmillennialism is proven wrong by our paradigm because that school, while admitting Matthew 24:14 was fulfilled in the first century, then insists Matthew 28 is another separate Commission. We have shown that to be false. The significance of this can hardly be over-emphasized. Gentry, in his definitive modern apology of postmillennialism explains the significance of the World Commission to postmillennialism: "It is important to note that the postmillennial view is the *only* one of the three major evangelical eschatologies that builds its case on the very charter for Christianity, the Great Commission."[63]

The futurist eschatology of postmillennialism is built upon the thesis of a yet future fulfillment of the Great Commission of Matthew 28. But the Commission of Matthew 28 and chapter 24 are *the identical Commission*. The postmillennialist admits that the Commission of Matthew 24 was fulfilled in the first century and that the eschatological significance of that Commission related to the end of the age in A. D. 70. This being true then to maintain a yet future eschatological application of the Great Commission the postmillennialist must take

What Does All This Mean?

the rather tenuous position that there was a hidden dual application to the end of the age in A.D. 70.

The postmillennialist must be able to prove several things to offset the implications of our paradigm:

1.] Prove that the Commission of Matthew 24 is different than the Commission of Matthew 13 or 28. Yet the identical words [ethne, nations] for the extent of the Commission are found in both chapter 24 and 28. In addition, we have shown the exact parallelism between Matthew 13 and 24 and pointed out that the postmillennialists apply Matthew 24 to the first century, e.g. Kik.

2.] Prove that Matthew 24 and Matthew 13 and 28 predicted two different ends of two different ages. These passages speak of the end of the age, [Mat. 13:39-40; 24:3; 28] and all use the identical and unusual term, *suntelias tou aionos*. To prove his point the postmillennialist must show that the identical term refers in Matthew 24 to the end of a Covenantal Age while in Matthew 13 and 28 it refers to the end of time. He must show that in chapters 13 and 28 it related to the destruction of material creation but in chapter 24 it meant Covenant Creation. He must show that in regard to the coming of the Lord at the end of the age, the coming of chapter 24 was spiritual but that in chapters 13 and 28 must refer to a literal return. That is a radical shift in meaning for the identical term used by the same author in the same book.

Chapters 24 and 28 also contain the promise of the miraculous gifts of the Spirit for the empowerment of the disciples as they fulfilled their mission, [Mk. 13:9ff; Mat. 28:20--"I am with you"]. This being true, the postmillennialist must become "charismatic" if Matthew 28 is yet to be fulfilled. Yet postmillennialist as a whole reject this view.[64]

3.] He must be able to prove that the first century eschatological significance of the Great Commission was simply a type or shadow of a still future eschatology. Yet not once did Jesus say the end of Israel's Covenant World foreshadowed something greater in significance.

What Does All This Mean?

In fact, he said that Israel's demise would be *the most significant cataclysm* that had occurred all the way back to creation or that ever would be, Mat. 24:21. He showed that the fall of Jerusalem was the time when he would be revealed in glory, Matthew 24:30, it would be the coming of the kingdom and redemption, Luke 21:28-31. The fall of Jerusalem was the time when the "children of Satan" and thus, Satan himself was finally defeated, John 8:44; Rev. 18-20. The Old Covenant of Death was finally removed, 2 Cor. 3. The Old Creation was destroyed, 2 Pet. 3, and the New Heavens and Earth, with the New Jerusalem were fully established, Rev. 21. The time of the judgment of the city "where the Lord was crucified" was the time when all the martyrs of God were to be vindicated, judged and rewarded, Mat. 23:29ff; Rev. 11:8f. It is difficult indeed therefore, to imagine that the fall of Jerusalem was foreshadowing something greater in the future.

We are convinced the postmillennialist is unable to prove any of

What Does All This Mean?

the above. We have shown that "the key continuity passage in scripture," Mat. 13, must be applied to the end of the Old Covenant Age in A. D. 70 after the completion of the World Commission. Thus, the postmillennial interpretation, grounded as it is in a futurist application of the Great Commission is impacted significantly by the first century fulfillment of the Commission.

Likewise, the **amillennial** view is shown to be in error because it too delineates between Matthew 24 and 28. Amillennialism says Matthew 24:14 definitely relates to the end of the age in A.D. 70 but Matthew 28 is totally unrelated to eschatology. But we have shown that in Matthew 24 Jesus *predicted* what would happen; in chapter 28 he *commanded* it to be done. In both texts the expectation is identical "the end of the age." Unless the amillennialist can produce definitive evidence for two ends of two ages separated so far by two millennia, then we must conclude that Matthew 24 and 28 speak of the identical "end of the age."

Since this is true, and since the pattern of *preaching, persecution, power, and parousia* permeates the entirety of the New Testament corpus this necessitates a total re-evaluation of the field of eschatology. Jesus did not predict an end of time; he predicted

A Call to Faith

the end of the Old Covenant World of Israel! That end came in the fall of Jerusalem in A.D. 70 just as he predicted!

  The purpose of this book is to provoke you to study; to encourage you to take inspiration seriously; to challenge you to reevaluate traditional concepts. We well understand that questions are raised about judgment, resurrection, etc., that are not covered in this work.[65] Other material is available that covers these topics extensively and shows that the coming of the Lord, judgment and resurrection are all indeed related to the end of the Old Covenant World in A.D. 70. We encourage you to obtain this material and study the subject further.

  The modern world is very much disillusioned with all the prophetic speculation that genders fear and uncertainty. The skeptics continue to have a field day with the fantastic but failed prognostications. Believers are continually disappointed by repeated failure of the "prophetic experts" who are so certain this must be the generation of Christ's return-- but it will not happen *because it has already happened*! It is time serious Bible students finally come to grips with the Bible

A Call to Faith

statements about *when* the end was to be and *what end* was predicted.

Bible eschatology is not about the end of history but the end of a Covenant History. Thus, *Covenant Eschatology*, not Historical Eschatology.

The Old Law was a world of death, 2 Cor. 3:6f; it could not give life, Gal. 3:20-21; Heb. 10:1-4. The Old Law was good for the purpose it was given, Gal. 3:22-24; Rom. 5:21, but it could not deliver from sin and death, Rom. 8:1-3.

God promised a New Covenant that could give life, Jer. 31:29-31; Rom. 8:1-3. That Old Covenant World would stand until it was *completely fulfilled*, Mat. 5:17-18, when the New Covenant was fully in place and matured. As the writer of Hebrews anticipated the perfection of the kingdom that was even then being delivered, 12:28, he said the Old Covenant was growing old and was now ready to vanish away, 8:13. The removal of that Old World was the removal of "heaven and earth" Heb. 12:25-27.

All of this is why the gospel had to be preached into all the world before the end. The New Covenant World had to be proclaimed and perfected before God removed the Old World. This is why the Great Commission is not about the end of the world and a literal coming of Christ.

A Call to Faith

Eschatology is about the end of that Old Covenant World and the revelation of Jesus in his New Covenant glory as King of Kings and Lord of Lords.

The detractors of the view set forth in this work claim that if Covenant Eschatology is true it destroys any reason for evangelism today.[66] For, say they, if all prophecy stands fulfilled and the Great Commission was fulfilled in the first century, there can be no reason for preaching today. This objection is shortsighted. Interestingly, these detractors provide the answers to their own objections!

Cates for instance says "As long as there are souls to be saved, the Great Commission of the church/kingdom will be in force"; and he adds "if the Gospel and the kingdom are eternal then it is necessarily the case that the kingdom and the Gospel **did not end** in A.D. 70!" [his emph.][67] He has destroyed his own objections!

Covenant Eschatology does not teach that the kingdom or the Gospel will ever be destroyed, nor does it teach that they ended in A.D. 70.[68] We teach that they were fully established/perfected/manifested in A.D. 70 and will stand forever "world without end" Eph. 3:21. Those who hold to an "end of time" eschatology, necessarily believe that evangelism will one day be terminated!

A Call to Faith

The time from Pentecost to A.D. 70 was a time of revelation and maturation, 1 Cor. 13; Eph. 4. But when the time of full maturation arrived at the parousia this was not to be the end of the proclamation of the Gospel but the time to proclaim from that time forward "the kingdoms of the world have become the kingdoms of our Lord and of His Christ" Rev. 11:15. It was the time to proclaim "mission accomplished" not "wait for another two or three, or more, millennia." It became the time to rejoice in salvation, not to wait any longer for it to be revealed, 1 Pet. 1:5-10. It was the time when resurrection life "in Christ" was fully revealed, Col. 3:1-4. It became the time when life outside of Christ was revealed for what it still is--death!

This is why Cates' own statement is one of the very reasons for the need to proclaim the Gospel today and forever, "As long as there are souls that need to be saved, the Great Commission of the church will be in force." The Gospel and the church *are without end*, and the task of the church is to proclaim perfected salvation in Christ. The Great Commission was fulfilled, the New Covenant World perfected. Christ has come as he said! And only if Jesus came can we trust the Bible. Only if he came can we trust *him* as Savior. Only if he came has the Old Covenant been removed, Mat. 5:17-18. Only if he came do we possess his New Covenant of eternal life. Only if he came do we possess the kingdom, Luke 21:31. Only if he came can we today dwell in the presence of God, Hebrews 9:6-10. Only if he came do we have salvation, Hebrews 9:28.

It is now the unending task of the church to proclaim the gospel "throughout all ages world without end" Eph. 3:20-21. It is time for the modern church to recognize the eschatological significance of the Great Commission *in the first century*, recognize that it was fulfilled, and stop generating false expectations and fears. It is time to stop preaching a partial salvation. It is time to stop proclaiming a "We have to keep on waiting for it" salvation. It is time to proclaim accomplished salvation in Christ!

TO CONTACT THE AUTHOR:
Don K. Preston
615 3rd N. W.
Ardmore, Ok. 73401
http://www.eschatology.org
or: DKPret@aol.com

Endnotes

1. A [dispensational] premillennialist is one who believes that national Israel remains as the chosen people of God and plays a central role in the future end time events. This involves the rebuilding of the Temple in Jerusalem, the restoration of the Old Covenant sacrificial system, the literal 1000 year reign of Christ on earth, and many other tenets including the Great Tribulation, the Man of Sin, etc. The millennialist does not believe that Christ established the kingdom because of the Jewish rejection of his mission. Instead, he established the church as an interim measure until his second coming in glory. In modern times the view has been popularized by Hal Lindsey's best-seller **The Late Great Planet Earth** and other books. For a fuller explanation see Dwight Pentecost's **Things To Come**, Zondervan, 1980.

2. Hal Lindsey, **There's A New World Coming**, Harvest House Publishers, 1973, p. 101.

3. An amillennialist is one who rejects the idea of a literal 1000 year reign of Christ. The 1000 year reign of Christ is understood figuratively of the entire Christian Age. The amillennialist believes that God was through with Israel at the Cross and that Christ's kingdom was fully established on Pentecost with the establishment of the church. It is held that the second coming of Christ will be to destroy earth and surrender the kingdom rule instead of to establish the kingdom in glory.

4. The postmillennialist believes that as a result of the completion of the World Mission sometime in the future "the overwhelming majority of men and nations will be

Christianized, righteousness will abound, wars will cease, and prosperity and safety will flourish." Kenneth Gentry, **He Shall Have Dominion**, Institute for Christian Economics, P. O. Box 8000, Tyler, Texas 75711, 1992, p. 71. At the end of this extended period of peace the Lord will return and destroy earth and history.

5. Franklin Camp, **The Work of the Holy Spirit**, Brothers, Inc. 4207 Adamsville Pkwy., Adamsville, Al. 35005. p. 82f.

6. Robert H. Smith, **History and Eschatology in Luke-Acts**, Vol. 29 [St. Louis: Concordia Publishing, 1958], 891-892.

7. Joseph Balyeat, **Babylon the Great City of Revelation**, OnWard Press, P. O. Box 4690, Sevierville, Tn. 37864, p. 217 1991. Balyeat is a postmillennialist.

8. Marcellus Kik, **Matthew XXIV**, Presbyterian and Reformed Publishing, Philadelphia, Penn. 1948, p. 42.

9. Beiderwolf, **The Second Coming Bible**, Baker, p. 347f.

10. Beiderwolf, p. 347.

11. William Bell, **This Generation** article in **The Living Presence**, Vol. 4, No. 4, Nov. 1993. 4705 Parkman Ave. N. W., Warren, Ohio, 44481

12. Exegetical Dictionary of the New Testament, Balz-Schneider, Eerdmans, 1990, Vol. 1, p. 241.

13. Hal Lindsey, **The Late Great Planet Earth**, Zondervan, 1974, p. 47.

14. "Gapology"--placing gaps of hundreds or thousands of years between verses is normally condemned by the amillennialist. Wayne Jackson for instance soundly condemns the premillennialist for finding such gaps:"the premillennialists have the unusual ability of finding 'gaps' where the Bible indicates none. They jam 2000 years between Isaiah 9:6 and 7; between Daniel 2:43 and 44, etc" **Studies in Hebrews**, Second Annual Denton Lectures, Valid Publications, 312 Pearl St. Denton, Tx. 76201, 1983, p. 510, n. #9. Strangely however, in note 21 he says that just because "Christ mentions his Second Coming in passages adjacent to Mark 9:1 and Matthew 16:28 does not necessarily identify the two as referring to the same event." Thus Jackson posits a gap of two thousand years in the period [.] between verse 27 and 28. This is the very thing he condemns in the millennial view!

15. A.T. Robertson, **Word Pictures in the New Testament**, Broadman, Vol. 1, 1930, p. 24

16. **The Analytical Greek Lexicon**, Zondervan, 1975, p. 262.

17. Donald Hagner, **Word Biblical Commentary**, Word Publishers, Dallas, Tx. 1993, p. 50.

18. Eusebius, **Ecclesiastical History**, Baker, 1987, p. 86.

19. **Encyclopedia Judaica Jerusalem**, MacMillan, Vol. 9., 1971, p. 1394.

20. For a discussion of the first century fulfillment of the Abomination of Desolation see Gary Demar's **Last Days Madness Obsession of the Modern Church**, American Vision Inc, 10 Perimeter Way, B-175, Atlanta, Ga. 30339.

21. See **The Second Coming Bible**, p. 492f, for a list of different views about the identity of the restrainer.

22. Oscar Cullman, Eschatology and Missions in the New Testament, in **The Background of the New Testament and its Eschatology**, edited by W. D. Davies and D. Daube, in honour of C. H. Dodd, Cambridge Press, 1956, p. 409f. Cullman actually built on the suggestion by Kummel.

23. On this see Johannes Munck, **Paul and the Salvation of Mankind,** John Knox Press, 1959.

24. James W. Thompson, **The Gentile Mission as an Eschatological Necessity,** Restoration Quarterly, Vol. 14, Number 1, First quarter, 1971, p. 18-27.

25. See **The Second Coming Bible**, Beiderwolf, p. 490.

26. G. R. Beasley-Murray, **Jesus and the Future**, MacMillan and Son, London, 1954, p. 260.

27. GARY NORTH VS. WES BREDENHOF: On the Kingdom of Christ in History (October 20, 1994), Part 1 of 3, an Internet exchange. North is a prominent postmillennialist associated with the Reconstructionist Movement.

28. Curtis Cates, 14th Annual Denton Lectureship, Pearl St. Church of Christ, 312 Pearl St. Denton, Tx. 76201. Open Forum Questions and Answers Tape.

29. Edward Wharton, **Christ and the Church,** Howard Publishing, West Monroe, La., 71291, 1992, p. 178.

30. Very plainly this parallelism has direct implications for the dating of Revelation.

31. See my book **2 Peter 3: The Late Great Kingdom** for a full vindication of this claim.

32. We have produced a MSS entitled **Who Is This Babylon?** in which we set forth a great deal of evidence to show that Babylon was indeed Jerusalem.

33. The traditional dating of 1 John is in the A.D. 90s. There is however, good evidence, both historical and Biblical, to support the view that all books of the New Testament were written before A.D. 70. See John A. T. Robinson's **Redating the New Testament**, Westminster Press, 1976 for a full discussion of this matter.

34. See the article **Marriage and Resurrection** by Max King in the Living Presence, Vol. 5, No. 11, June 1995. 4705 Parkman Rd. N. W., Warren, Ohio, 44481. This is an excellent exposition of Luke 20 showing that the "this age" and "that age" contrast is between the Old Covenant World and the New Covenant World.

35. Max King, **Living Presence,** op. cit.

36. **Have Heaven and Earth Passed Away**? available from us.

37. **Englishman's Greek Concordance**, Zondervan, 1976, p. 181f.

38. Dwight Pentecost, **Things To Come**, Zondervan, 1958, p. 463f.

39. See Wayne Jackson, "the law was abrogated at the Cross." Annual Denton Lectureship Book 1983, Valid Publications, 312 Pearl St. Denton, Tx. 76201.

40. See our book **Seal Up Vision and Prophecy: A Study of the Seventy Weeks of Daniel 9** for a demonstration that the fall of Jerusalem would be the time and event wherein all prophecy was finally fulfilled.

41. See John R. McRay, **To Telion in 1 Corinthians 13:10,** Restoration Quarterly, P. O. Box 8227 Station ACC Abilene, Tx., 79601, Vol. 14, Num. 3 and 4, Third and Fourth Quarter, 1971, p. 168f. McRay shows in a powerful way that "the perfect" referred to Jew and Gentile equality. This view has dramatic and far reaching implications for the cessation of miracles, the Day of the Lord, the dating of the New Testament books and other issues that space will not allow us to explore.

42. Franklin Camp, **Work,** p. 179.

43. Fred O. Francis, **Eschatology and History in Luke-Acts,** Journal of the American Academy of Religion, 37, 1969, pp. 49-63.

44. J.D. Bales, **Hub of the Bible**, Old Paths Book Club, p. 68.

45. A. J. Mattill, **Luke and Last Things**, Western Carolina Press, 1979, p. 102.

46. Anthony Hoekema, **The Bible and The Future**, Eerdmans, pp. 55-67.

47. Yet Hoekema says the scriptural evidence suggests "that miraculous gifts of the Spirit, such as glossolalia, are no longer present in the church today." Hoekema, **What About Tongue Speaking?** Eerdmans, 1973, p. 113.

48. George Eldon Ladd, **A Theology of the New Testament**, Eerdmans, 1974, p. 343.

49. O. Palmer Robertson, **Tongues: Sign of Covenantal Curse and Blessing**, Westminster Theological Journal, Philadelphia, vol. 38, 1975, p. 45-53.

50. David Chilton, **Paradise Restored**, Dominion Press, Ft. Worth, Tx., 1987, p. 118.

51. Gary North, **Christian Reconstruction**, Vol. XX, No. 1, Jan/Feb. 1996, P. O. Box 8000, Tyler, Tx. 75711.

52. This would include amillennialists, premillennialists and postmillennialists! All three schools are, to varying degrees, opposed to the charismatic claims. There are of course exceptions within these schools.

53. See our tract **Can You Believe Jesus Said This?!?** for a fuller discussion of this text.

54. See our book **Second Peter Three: The Late Great Kingdom** for a full discussion of the use of figurative language in prophecy.

55. Paul S. Minear, **New Testament Apocalyptic**, Abingdon, 1981, p. 52-53.

56. Curtis Cates, **The A.D. 70 Theology**, Cates Publishing, 9194 Lakeside Dr. Olive Branch, MS., 38654, 1995, p. 26-27.

57. See for instance Wayne Jackson, **The A. D. 70 Theory: A Review of the Max King Doctrine**, 1990, P.O. Box 55265, Stockton, Calif. p. 28-32.

58. Scholars have long recognized that Paul's eschatology in Thessalonians is drawn from the Old Testament and the Olivet Discourse. G.R. Beasley-Murray, **Jesus and the Future**, p. 232-233; David Wenham, **Paul and the Synoptic Apocalypse**, in **Gospel Perspectives: Studies of History and Tradition in the Four Gospel**, JSOT Press, Sheffield, England, edited by R.T. France and David Wenham, Vol. II, 1981, pp. 345-375; and, G. Henry Watterman, **The Sources of Paul's Teaching on the 2nd Coming of Christ in 1 and 2nd Thessalonians**, Journal of the Evangelical Theological Society Vol. 18, 1975, pp. 105-113.

59. See our **Who Is This Babylon?** referenced above.

60. David Chilton, **Paradise Restored**, p. 200.

61. David Chilton, **Days of Vengeance**, Dominion Press, 1987, p. 361f.

62. Pentecost, **Things To Come**, p. 463f.

63. Kenneth Gentry, **He Shall Have Dominion**, Institute for Christian Economics, Tyler, Texas, 1992, p. 233.

64. See Kenneth Gentry's **The Charismatic Gift of Prophecy**, FootStool Publications, P.O. BOX 161021 Memphis, Tn. 38186, 1989.

65. For a comprehensive discussion of these subjects see Max R. King's work **The Cross and the Parousia**, a scholarly presentation of "Covenant Eschatology." The book may be purchased from Great Christian Books, 229 S. Bridge St. Elkton, Md. 21922-8000. Contact us for a list of other materials available.

66. Cates, **Theology**, p. 79-80.

67. Cates argues: The church and gospel are *eternal*, therefore the church and gospel continued in force beyond A.D. 70. But turn this around: the church and gospel are eternal, therefore the church and the gospel will continue in force beyond the "end of time." Either Cates' "end of time" eschatology is wrong or there will be evangelism after the "end of time."

68. Cates' accusations in this regard are blatantly false and totally misrepresent the views of advocates of Realized Eschatology. But his book is full of such misrepresentations and half truths.